Into the Open

Into the Open

. . .

Reflections on Genius and Modernity

. . .

Benjamin Taylor

New York University Press
New York and London

NEW YORK UNIVERSITY PRESS
New York and London

Library of Congress Cataloging-in-Publication Data
Taylor, Benjamin, 1952–
    Into the open : reflections on genius and modernity /
Benjamin Taylor.
        p. cm.
    Includes bibliographical references and index.
    ISBN 0–8147–8213–2
    1. Gifted person—Case studies. 2. Genius—Case
studies. 3. Pater, Walter, 1839–1894. 4. Valéry, Paul,
1871–1945. 5. Freud, Sigmund, 1856–1939. I. Title.
BF416.A1T38 1995
155.9'8—dc20   94–41349
                    CIP

New York University Press books are printed on acid-free
paper, and their binding materials are chosen for strength
and durability.

Manufactured in the United States of America

10 9 8 7 6 5 4 3 2 1

• • •

To A. T. and S. T., who provided.

· · ·

There is basically only one problem in the world and it is this: how do you break through? How do you get out into the open?
—Adrian Leverkühn, in Thomas Mann's *Doctor Faustus*

Contents

* * *

Acknowledgments

Long ago, on a walk from Ezra Stiles College to Sterling Library, Harold Bloom helped me to find out what was murkily on my mind. I was no student at Yale, just an importuning stranger. It is a pleasure now to thank Professor Bloom for that first nudge toward this book.

At Columbia Carl Woodring and Frank Kermode directed my doctoral research with wisdom and vigilance and friendliness. I had, in addition, the benefit of unsparing criticisms from Edward W. Said.

I got on terms, after graduate school, with three great books, Czeslaw Milosz's *The Land of Ulro*, Leszek Kolakowski's *Modernity on Endless Trial*, and George Steiner's *Real Presences*—our most powerful accounts of the modern, I would say. All I had thought required rethinking after I read them, and my work is a dinghy in the wake of these big ships.

An earlier version of Chapter 1 appeared in *Raritan*, and I am indebted to editors of that quarterly for helpful advice. The late Howard Moss suggested improvements to a draft of Chapter 2. Richard Howard, Daniel Shea, Joel Conarroe, Frances Kiernan, Peter Matson, Jeannette Haien, David Hadas, Sanford Friedman, Naomi Lebowitz, Amy Hempel, and Leonard Barkan have been particular friends to *Into the Open*, as to me, and I shall always be grateful with love to them.

The late Sondra J. Stang, a mighty example of how to study

and how to live, taught me much in the too few years I knew her.

Despina Papazoglou Gimbel, an exacting editor, has saved me often from myself in what follows. I am obliged to her and also to Jennifer Hammer and David Updike for assistance in seeing the book to print. It is a pleasure to acknowledge Colin Jones's good counsel. Profoundest thanks go lastly to Carlton Rochell, my publisher, for all his faith and works.

Memorial Day, 1994
East Hampton, New York

Introduction: We Romantics

Now, Ariel, I am that I am, your late and lonely master,
  Who knows now what magic is:—the power to enchant
That comes from disillusion.

—W. H. Auden

Start with *Animal Crackers*, the scene where Chico and Harpo accost a Mr. Roscoe W. Chandler—hair brilliantined and mustache twitching, fair game for the Marxist excoriation.

"I'm-a know you from-a somewhere," Chico says.

"My good man," replies Chandler, "there must be a mistake."

"I'm a-know you, I'm-a know you, just-a let me see. Now I'm-a remember. You are Aby the feesh peddler from Czechoslowakia."

"Preposterous! Fantastic! An outrage!" Chandler cries.

"Aby, and here's the proof: you got on-a your arm a beeg boythmark."

With help from Harpo, Chico throws the man of doubtful identity to the ground and rips off the sleeve of his swallowtail coat to disclose a large unpleasant birthmark. Here Roscoe Chandler bursts into sobs, breaks down completely, bawling to Chico in a heavy Yiddish accent: "You're right,

1

I'm Aby! It was a long time ago! Look, we can maybe keep
this between us? How much you want? I'm a rich man, I can
pay you!"

He offers Chico and Harpo everything. They'll have none
of it. Chico sets up a taunting cry: "Aby, the *feesh* man! Aby,
the *feesh* man!" Harpo honks his horn for joy.

Jeering thus at Roscoe Chandler, they express an essential
of our modernity—the nihilistic gesture, the unmasking of
what is "higher." As a young graduate chameleon, wishing
to be as modern as could be, I'd read the wise men of the
moment and taken a nihilistic coloring from what they had
to say. Hell, I wanted to be a good Nietzschean too, so I
resolved to unmask something—the received notion of genius. A mere cultural construct, I jeered. A Romantic ideology. But genius had a way of jeering back. Make sense of art
or science without me, the cultural construct said. And I
realized, at length, that I could not. What was "higher"
turned out not to be a cover for something else; what was
"higher" turned out to be higher. Thus I arrived at my conclusion, which I state here at the outset: genius, the Romantic idea of man transcending himself, is what we cannot not
believe in.

I mean that a humanistic faith in genius remains, despite
the lateness of the day, as spontaneous to us as were the
covenantal faiths of *halakhah* or of Word-made-flesh to our
ancestors. This is not, of course, to suggest that humanistic
faith is equal to religious faith. Dante Alighieri did not possess the word "genius" in our modern sense, nor did he need
it. He called Aristotle "master of all men who know." He
called Virgil "light and honor of all poets." We would call
them geniuses, implying that they are cases of man transcending himself, escaping the taint of ordinariness. But it
should be remembered that the "master of all who know"
and the "light of all poets" remain, according to Dante, perpetual prisoners of themselves, residents of Hell despite their
greatness, the one true way of exoneration being by a route

unavailable to them. Man transcends man, according to Dante, through the grace brought about by Christ's death and resurrection—by that way and no other. We post-traditional men and women are modern precisely because we do not believe things like this. But it may be useful, calling ourselves modern, to think back on the old word for what we are—apostate. Consider in this light Simon Magus, father of apostasy, father of us all insofar as we are modern, who bade defiance to Christian miracles with a wizardry of his own:

There was a certain man, called Simon, which beforetime in the same city used sorcery, and bewitched the people of Samaria, giving out that himself was some great one: To whom they all gave heed, from the least to the greatest, saying, this man is the great power of God. And to him they had regard, because that of long time he had bewitched them with sorceries.[1]

Those among us who are good Nietzscheans have, in effect, proposed an analogy between ourselves and these Samaritans, heeders of the mage. We moderns, too, have been laid under a spell, so the argument goes. We moderns, no less than our cultural ancestors, have carved tablets of law and declared them sacred truths, believed in something rather than nothing. In this are we different from those who've gone before us: Greeks, Persians, Hebrews, Romans, Gnostics, Christians? As the form of spirit supervening on these others, Romanticism—the characteristic modern consciousness— has stood no less than its predecessors for

a suddenly erupting decision in favor of ignorance, of deliberate exclusion, a shutting of one's windows, an internal No to this or that thing, a refusal to let things approach, a kind of state of defense against much that is knowable, a satisfaction with the dark, a Yea and Amen to ignorance.[2]

Successively, down the ages, what have we defended ourselves against? *Nihilism*, the uncanny guest Nietzsche perceived at Europe's door. What is it? Denial of the existence of higher values, of any truthful world (Platonic *physis*, the Hebraic God, the Christian Word-made-flesh, the Gnostic *pneuma*, the Romantic sublime), of any beyond or in-itself exonerated from the shadow play of what Platonists call becoming, Jews and Christians call history, Gnostics call creation, and Romantics call the universe of death—each an alien element from which you must get yourself redeemed. Such has been the Platonic, Jewish, Christian, Gnostic, or Romantic aim of life. And precisely here lies the difference between all these and that which is, according to Nietzsche, their necessary successor and ultimate consequence: "What does nihilism mean?" he asks. "*That the highest values devaluate themselves*. The aim is lacking; 'why?' finds no answer."[3] Nietzsche understood the history of man's highest or redemptive values (call them tablets of overcoming, sacred truths) as so many decisions in favor of ignorance—fondly mistaken for truth, but which Nietzschean psychology unmasks as expressions of the fundamental requirement for *untruth*, the metaphysical need not to be without answers to the answerless questions. There are only interpretations, he declares—which we mistake for verities; the task of his psychology is to unmask these as bewitchments, spells, Yeas and Amens to ignorance. The sacred beliefs a culture propounds Nietzsche would expose as its *sacred delusions*.

Simon Magus must, from the Nietzschean perspective, be granted his due for having retailed a gospel (even if a failed one) inimical to that of the primitive church. In the end, orthodox Christianity not Gnosticism gained the day, as everybody knows. Simon and his tidings endured a long occultation. But if history cast him down, it did not throw him out. He skulked through all the centuries, waiting with his message—for us apostates, us Romantics, us moderns.

A little is known about him, much more figmented. The individual of that name who turns up in Irenaeus and in the paleographic finds at Nag Hammadi may or may not be the same Simon who bewitched Samaritans in the Book of Acts.

What we can say with certainty is that there is a Simon Magus associated early on with Gnostic doctrines of the maleficence of all creation; of an evil demiurge as universal instigator; of a Plenitude which lies beyond the demiurge and of which the demiurge knows nothing; and last, of a path of saving knowledge or *gnosis,* a way out of this acosmic abortion and back to the true unknown God. Thus the teachings of Gnosticism, which, various though they are, some heterodoxly Christian, others Jewish, still others pagan, do have in common the stress on ignorance versus enlightenment, deficiency versus fulfillment—not sin versus repentance. According to orthodox Christianity our birthright was squandered in Eden and only through grace can we regain it. According to Gnosticism, by contrast, the human mind and heart possess boundless unhampered means, redeem themselves without benefit of the divine revelation. Gnostic disclosures are, invariably, of the godhead within. Simon Magus affirms that in every human being "dwells an infinite power . . . the root of the universe."[4] Craving for knowledge leads the *pneumatikos* or spiritualized man—who is to Gnosticism what the saint is to orthodox Christianity—upward from bondage to his redemption. A vehement impulse to know, and not the inclined heart made whole and capable of faith through God's gift of grace, gains him his release. The Gnostic beholds no impediment of sin. He therefore feels no need for God's propitiation. Among Nag Hammadi texts, the *Testimony of Truth* defines the Gnostic as "a disciple of his own mind,"[5] whose goal is the liberating discovery that he— and not that evil demiurge whom the many have mistaken for divine—is the sole source of truth. Similarly, a text called the *Book of Thomas the Contender* declares that "whoever has not known himself has known nothing, but he who has known himself has at the same time already achieved knowledge about the depths of all things."[6] And the Gnostic Jesus of the *Gospel of Thomas* puts it, very succinctly, like this: "If you bring forth what is within you, what you bring forth

will save you."[7] Self and God turn out to be identical, once
the doors of perception have been cleansed. According to
Gnosticism, man has still a great birthright—not forfeit in
Eden but rather eclipsed in the original catastrophe of creation. Original sin? It is the demiurge, not ourselves, who is
primordially at fault. The Gnostic or "knowing one" reaches
back of the demiurge's botched handiwork to reclaim fulfillment. This is *gnosis*, the transport of knowledge that
makes of him, according to the *Gospel of Philip*, "no longer a
Christian, but a Christ."[8] *Gnosis* equates the knower to God,
as does neither faith nor salvation in orthodox Christianity.
What the texts of Nag Hammadi compel us to acknowledge
is a fierce and original *humanism* of the first and second
centuries, which the emergent catholic church rightly recognized as inimical to its own creed and hazardous to its authority. This humanism, like any other, ascribes to man sufficient greatness to make his own way out of the dark. Here I
will venture a generalization and say that according to every
humanism there is an inward vehemence for knowledge—
what the Germans call a *Wissensdrang*—by which man
works out his redemption. If this sounds too obviously Faustian to be applicable to the Gnostics, it is well to recall that
when in Rome our Simon Magus, father of apostasy, went by
the nom de guerre of Faustus—literally, "the favored one."[9]
Was the notorious early-sixteenth-century black magician
and sodomite who called himself Doctor Faustus, and whose
exploits were reported at Kreuznach, Heidelberg, Erfurt, In-
golstadt, Münster, and elsewhere, by his own choice a name-
sake of the Magus? Or was the name given him by others?
We don't really know, and in either case the implications are
clear enough. Here was a purveyor, in the grand tradition, of
forbidden things. If overshadowed in his own day by more
renowned alchemists (Tritheim, Paracelsus, Agrippa von
Nettlesheim, Nostradamus) it was nonetheless Faustus who
posthumously emerged in the popular folkbooks, the puppet
plays, the ecclesiastical lore, and the literature as embodi-

ment of an interdicted *Wissensdrang*. The devil, too, has his anointed ones, Christianity had declared long since: *Habet diabolus christos suos*, and worth mentioning in this connection is that the Manichean sage whom Saint Augustine so ardently awaits in book 5 of the *Confessions*, and by whom he is so miserably let down, called himself Faustus too. The German Faustus inherits this legacy of the devil's anointed ones, damned like his predecessors in the shameless hungry quest to do and know, until transfigured by Lessing and Goethe in the second half of the eighteenth century. Only with them does the Faustian *Wissensdrang* become a path of salvation. The Faust who emerges into the light, crying "Hier ist es Zeit, durch Taten zu beweisen, Dass manneswürde nicht der Götterhöhe weich" (The time has come to prove by deeds that mortals have as much dignity as God) is no bounden agent of evil, but instead the heroic embodiment of a humanistic rage to know.

Orthodox Christian accounts, eager to discredit Simon Magus, ancient original of Faust, had reported on a flying exhibition he gave for the Emperor Nero. It is said that while Simon did manage to get aloft, he as surely fell like a plummet back to earth. Another account has it that he allowed himself to be buried alive, expecting to rise on the third day. Such was the idea of the mage bequeathed to the Christian Middle Ages. He was evil, or impotent, or both by turns: a conjurer, a necromancer, a fake. To be sure, Renaissance culture, first in Italy and later in transalpine Europe, challenged this wholesale contempt for magic. Over against the filthy doings of Sycorax, the Renaissance acknowledged Prospero's book and staff. Here is how Giovanni Pico della Mirandola, greatest of quattrocento humanists, puts the matter, distinguishing black from white:

Just as that first form of magic makes a man a slave and pawn of evil powers, the latter makes him their lord and master. The first form of magic cannot justify any claim to being either an art or a science while the latter, filled as it is with mysteries, embraces the most profound contemplation of the deepest secrets of things and finally the knowledge of the whole of nature. This beneficent magic, in calling forth, as it were, from their hiding places into the light the powers which the largess of God has sown and planted in the world, does not itself work miracles, so much as sedulously serve nature as she works her wonders.[10]

Magic is, for Pico, "a higher and holier philosophy"[11]—"the highest realization of natural philosophy."[12] The white magician conjures no demons from below; to the contrary, he summons influences from above, making marriage thereby of the timebound to the sempiternal: "As the farmer weds his elms to the vines, so the magus marries earth to heaven," says Pico, "that is to say, the forces of inferior things to the gifts and properties of supernal things."[13] Hence his services to creation. The white magician's *Wissensdrang* enables a great conciliation of ourselves to God. He is, says Pico, "the minister of nature and not merely its artful imitator."[14]

Of course, Pico's revaluation of magic forms part of a large-scale revaluation of man which we associate with the fifteenth-century Italian revival of learning and, in particular, of neoplatonic philosophy. It was then, as I've indicated, that magic shed its old disedifying character. So far from implying demonic assistance, as before, magical practices could be taken as proof of a superior knowledge of the interlocking and all-pervading forces in nature. It has been a question of scholarly interest whether Leonardo da Vinci, Pico's elder Florentine contemporary, understood his work—as scientist and artist, artist and scientist, each endeavor serving the other—in neoplatonic and magical terms. We know of da Vinci's contempt for "alchemists, necromancers and other ingenious simpletons," as he scathingly puts it. We know also that he believed "the painter's mind must of necessity transform itself into the very mind of nature, . . . must be able to expound the causes of the manifestations of her laws."[15] Nature becomes available to Leonardo's art only on condition that she is grasped in her inner necessity. The marvels are there—in the things of the world being as they are and not some other way, and in their amenability to knowledge. He regarded his art, based on the very mind of nature, as the only real magic. And he placed painting first among human pursuits because it furnished the synthesis of all the distinctive activities of the mind; because it vouchsafed a conclusion to scientific problems, showed forth the "marvelous" and "stupendous" necessity compelling each observable effect to be the direct result of its cause. In order to paint the truth, the visual truth, his explorations pierced through to unseen *ragioni* of experience. In order to depict appearances, Leonardo researched causes. Happy the man who knows these. But happier still he who makes them manifest in an image, thereby reconciling the unknown to the known. Leonardo's notebooks, chaotic though they are, imply a unitary view of reality—grounded in mechanical principles and susceptible of mathematical expression. Whereas we would call this perspective technological or scientific, the Italian fifteenth century was more apt to regard it as *magical,* and no scholar has come nearer the quick of the da Vinci question than Kenneth Clark when he writes,

Just as Leonardo, in his pursuit of natural forces, hung on with a kind of inspired tenacity, so in the St. John we feel him pressing closer round the form, penetrating further and further into the mystery, till at last he seems to become a part of it so that, like his contemporaries, we no longer think of him as a scientist, a seeker after measurable truth, but as a magician, a man who, from close familiarity with the processes of nature, has learnt a disturbing secret of creation.[16]

The magician knows things we others cannot know. Such powers the Renaissance regarded as proof of his *ingenium*— his nature, not his nurture. To possess secrets of creation was a destiny, revealed early on. Accordingly, in Vasari's *Lives of the Artists* a peasant boy named Giotto leaves off herding his father's sheep to draw pictures of them on the rocks. Along comes Cimabue and, knowing at a glance the glory and promise of the child, takes him in hand. Vasari emphasizes, in the general preface to his *Lives*, an inexplicable impulse or force of nature behind great artistic careers, an untutored *invenzione*, manifest from youth and accompanying the artist throughout his life. The old in-born gifts of divine inspiration which antiquity had ascribed to the poet, Renaissance Italy extends to the great painters and sculptors. Vasari speaks of a *furore dell'arte*, a creative ecstasy transfiguring rather than just copying the world. Thus the artist proves himself a second god—*alter deus*, as Alberti had already in the quattrocento put it.

Legend says that while still a boy Leonardo sculpted terracotta heads that seemed the work of a great artist. His father Ser Piero took him to Florence and apprenticed him to Andrea del Verrochio, in whose *bottega* Leonardo even as a journeyman shamed the master, adding to *Saint John Baptising Christ* an angel that rendered the rest of the painting commonplace by comparison. Legend says, further, that Verrochio could never again bring himself to take up brush and palette.

We know that throughout Leonardo's life such myths of the inexplicable go on accruing to him, and culminate after his death in Vasari's "miraculous and heavenly" Maestro who, dissatisfied merely to represent nature, debates and competes with her and makes himself, finally, master of her, having acquired secret and total comprehension of her ways. So when, in the 1850s, the historian Michelet refers to da Vinci as "the Italian brother of Faust,"[17] he is invoking a supernatural sense of him that is certainly not new. Only the doing and knowing of all things could satisfy Leonardo, as only the doing and knowing of all things can redeem Faust.

Only the breaching of every boundary grants fulfillment, confers the true mastery.

Pico had written that man's dignity was the result of his freedom to make an essence of his own rather than being assigned one. "I have given you," says God in the *Oration on the Dignity of Man*,

no fixed abode, and no visage of your own, nor any special gift, in order that whatever place or aspect or talents you yourself will have desired, you may have and possess them wholly in accord with your desire and your own decision. Other species are confined to a prescribed nature, under laws of my making. No limits have been imposed upon you, however; you determine your nature by your own free will, in the hands of which I have placed you. I have placed you at the world's very center, that you may better behold from this point whatever is in the world. And I have made you neither celestial or terrestrial, neither mortal nor immortal, so that, like yourself, you may mold yourself wholly in the form of your choice.[18]

Who is man? The indeterminate creature, whose dignity is his freedom to do or be anything. Who, then, is man as mage? The maestro of nature, the limit case of greatness. Such is the mystery Leonardo's *Wissensdrang* came to stand for.

It still does. But we Romantics have given the mystery a new name. The Renaissance had its magi, we have had our *geniuses*. These latter continue by new means an old myth of the unaccountable. The genius, as Nietzsche puts it early in his career, "augments nature with new living nature."[19] There is in this the echo of a predecessor. His early master, Schopenhauer, had written in *Parerga and Paralipomena* that the

intellectual life, like some gift from heaven, hovers over the stir and movement of the world; or it is, as it were, a sweet-scented air developed out of the ferment itself—the real life of mankind, dominated by will; and side by side with the history of nations, the history of philosophy, science and art takes its bloodless way. . . . It happens only now and then, let us say once in a century, that a man is born whose intellect so perceptibly surpasses the normal measure as to amount to a second faculty which seems accidental, as it is out of all relation to the will. He may remain a long time without being recognized or appreciated, stupidity preventing the one and envy the other. But should this once come to pass, mankind will crowd round him and his works, in the hope that he may be able to enlighten some of the darkness of their existence or inform them about it. . . . A man of learning is a man who has learned a great deal; a man of genius, one from whom we learn something which the genius has learned from nobody. Great minds, of which there are scarcely one in a hundred million, are thus the lighthouses of humanity; and without them mankind would lose itself in a boundless sea of monstrous error and bewilderment. The simple man of learning, in the strict sense of the word—the ordinary professor, for instance—looks upon a genius much as we look upon a hare, which is good to eat once it has been killed and dressed, but alive is only good to shoot at. . . . Those who emerge from the multitude, those who are called men of genius, are the *lucida intervalla* of the whole human race.[20]

These continue by new means an old myth of the unaccountable. Man is a great miracle; man as genius, creating after the prototype of God, the greatest miracle of all.

Genius: *génie* in French, *Genie* in German, *genio* in Italian. From a pair of Latin words—*genius*, meaning the guardian spirit of a family or an individual; and *ingenium*, meaning the inborn capacity or natural aptitude that is prior to technical training. Both have their root in the verb *gignere*, to beget, akin to the Greek *gignesthai*, to be born, to come into being. Since the first quarter of the eighteenth century "genius" has chiefly signified native intellectual or artistic power of an exalted kind, miraculous creative capacity as distinct from talent. In English as in the other vernacular languages, the word first indicated tutelary spirits connected to a place, institution, or way of life. "Genius" was subsequently employed, at least from the seventeenth century, to denote the presiding gifts of a particular nation or epoch.

Hence, through a further innovation, it came to mean the natural quality of mind suiting an individual to a given task. In Addison's essay number 160 in *The Spectator,* dated 1711, we find the distinction—more and more familiar as the eighteenth century progresses—between those who create out of an inexplicable natural endowment and those who work only by means of art or learning. In response to French neoclassicism Englishmen will point to the great irregular poetry of their chief national writer—snatching "Grace beyond the Reach of Art," Pope said—as a case incommensurate with every received norm. (Indeed, it is above all in eighteenth-century Shakespeare criticism that the triumph over neoclassical constraint will be won and that the idea of the individual of genius, creating as if another God, will become customary parlance.) Dr. Johnson's *Dictionary* of 1755 offers, alongside older and variously moldered meanings of the word "genius," a tame formula for our characteristic modern acceptation—one "endowed with superior faculties." Four years later, Edward Young in his *Conjectures on Original Composition* will speak more with the true voice of the age: "Learning we thank, Genius we revere: That gives us pleasure, This gives us rapture; That informs, This inspires; and is itself inspired; for genius is from heaven, learning from man."

The influence of Young on important continental figures was rapid, part of a general wearing down of received neoclassical standards. We find, for example, the echo of him in Diderot's 1765 entry for "genius" in the *Encyclopédie:*

The man of *génie* is he whose ranging soul occupies itself with all that is in nature, receiving from her no idea that is not roused by his distinctive play of emotion. All is brought to life, turned to account; nothing is lost, nothing wasted. . . . He casts upon nature an eye gifted for the comprehension of abysses. . . . As for his constructs, they are too audacious for ordinary reason to inhabit. . . . In the arts as in the sciences . . . the genius seems to change the very nature of things; his character envelops whatever it touches; he casts into the future his piercing lights; he leaps ahead of his century, and it is powerless to follow him. He leaves behind those intellects which seek, even rightly, as may be, to criticize—poor lockstepped minds which leave nature as they found it. Behold him they may but are powerless to know him. For the genius alone may tell us truly who and what he is.[21]

In German cultural life, owing partly to the influence of Young and other authors imported from England, the role of *genie* was immense in the late eighteenth and early nineteenth centuries. Sturm und Drang was known also to Germans as the *Genieperiode* or era of genius. Under this sign, Shakespeare was belatedly discovered to them. The prodigal figure of Goethe, growing old and universal, became synonymous with *Genie* in all its forms. As previous cultures had taken their bearings from the hero, the prophet, the *pneumatikos*, the saint, so Germany in the period of highest achievement and influence took its bearings from the genius, who was *Mustermensch der Menschlichkeit gegenüber*.

These are Goethe's words to describe Leonardo da Vinci. The Maestro is the measure of true humanity, Goethe declares. The Maestro and his *Wissensdrang* are what are most real. In Goethe's formulation we already find much of what Schopenhauer has to say about genius in the *Parerga*. And we hear again this original Goethean sense of genius, now mediated by Schopenhauer, in the young Nietzsche speaking of "men to whom the whole of nature is impelled for its redemption"—a phrase from *Schopenhauer as Educator* (1874), third of the *Untimely Meditations*.

But in Nietzsche's subsequent work that Goethean and Schopenhauerian legacy—the genius as *Mustermensch der Menschlichkeit gegenüber*—gets unmasked, Roscoe Chandler shown up, as it were, for Aby the fishmonger. The Nietzsche of the middle or so-called positivist period—from *Human, All Too Human* (1878) to *The Gay Science* (1882)—casts away genius, finding it a Romantic relic inconsistent with his thoroughgoing skepticism. He argues that we Romantics have wrongly bestowed our reverence. "If we consider all that has been hitherto revered as 'superhuman mind,' as 'genius,' " he writes,

> we come to the sad conclusion that the intellectuality of mankind must have been something very low and paltry. . . . The great human being is still, in precisely the greatest thing that demands reverence, invisible like a too distant star. . . . The order of rank of greatness for all past mankind has not yet been determined.[22]

Nietzsche looks ahead to a transvaluation of values that will obviate, along with all metaphysical need, our *Geniebedürfnis* or need for genius. From the vantage point of that transvaluation—he calls it the overman—all greatness hitherto, all the most resplendent *Wissensdränge* we have known, shall be disclosed as not-yet and not-enough. The overman will laugh from the height of a distant star at our Romantic need for genius, much as he will laugh at our fantasies of a creator God; and of the unique and immortal soul he has granted to each of us; and of the freedom of each to live a life of response to his grace or not. The overman will repudiate all these consoling old thoughts in favor of a new one that consoles not at all:

> What, if some day or night a demon were to steal after you into your loneliest loneliness and say to you: "This life as you now live it and have lived it, you will have to live once more and innumerable times more; and there will be nothing new in it, but every pain and every joy and every thought and sigh and everything unutterably small or great in your life will have to return to you, all in the same succession and sequence—even this spider and this moonlight between the trees, and even this moment and I myself. The eternal hourglass of existence is turned upside down again and again, and you with it, speck of dust."[23]

Nihilism can be no completer than this. Eternal recurrence of the same means: omnipotence of the nil, eternally. This

Nietzschean mandala of meaninglessness—most difficult and dangerous and destructive of thoughts, thinkable only by the *Übermensch*—makes bombast of the dignity of man, predicated as that Renaissance teaching is, according to Nietzsche, on our delusions of free will. For where is the *liberum arbitrium* in a speck of dust? Nietzsche, hard-set enemy of all humanisms, Gnostic or Renaissance or Romantic, thinks his way through to a nullity of will raised to the highest power. Nothing could be deadlier to the fantasies of humanism than eternal recurrence of the same; no determinism could be more crushing.

Has not this thought experiment (a better term for eternal recurrence than argument, doctrine, or teaching, for it is really none of these) remained our furthest venture into what is called the "decentering of the subject"? Nietzsche announced himself Europe's first perfect nihilist, ruiner of a sacred Romantic truth—the idea of genius. Taking the limit case of him for my control, I will examine three rather more anxious, less perfect representatives of modernity—Walter Pater, Paul Valéry, and Sigmund Freud. Leonardo da Vinci becomes a problem for each of these because the received sense of genius, of selfhood at its highest reach, has for each been so deeply, if implicitly, called into question. Called into question, I emphasize; but not repudiated. To the query, "How do you get out into the open?" the propounder of eternal recurrence would shout out, "You don't!" Nietzsche, Europe's first perfect nihilist, exulted in *the unselving of man*; it is an exultation in which Pater, Valéry, and Freud refuse to share, although the process of unselving, the waning of the Romantic, is as inherent to their work as it is programmatic in Nietzsche's. The elated Romantic humanism from which our modern notion of genius was bred palls here to uncertainty. For Pater, Valéry, and Freud, Leonardo is a means of confronting what modernity has taken from us. Each answers the question, "How do you break through?" with a vexed and reluctant "You don't." Each acknowledges *a marginality of personal volition,* each makes of *encumberment* the abiding metaphor. Yet they do not venture so far as Nietzsche; they do not relinquish the idea of genius, hedged about though it is in their works by skepticism. Pater, Valéry, and Freud remain equivocal, troubled witnesses. We may study in them the encroachments of an uncanny guest into our long-lived culture of Romanticism.

Chapter 1

Walter Pater's Eucharist

But how does one feel?
One grows used to the weather,
The landscape and that;
And the sublime comes down
To the spirit itself,

The spirit and space,
The empty spirit
in vacant space.
What wine does one drink?
What bread does one eat?
—Wallace Stevens

What would be fun, declared the undergraduate Pater, would be to get oneself ordained and not believe a word of it. And he would have acted on the impulse had not a devout classmate, alert to Pater's mischief, forestalled him with letters to the Bishop of London.

Callow as it is, the episode furnishes us with a clue. Having put aside the Christian pieties of a boyhood spent in the cathedral school at Canterbury, Pater kept an admiration for the High Church liturgy. What the pious youth had sought in Canterbury Cathedral, the mature agnostic would seek again in Brasenose Chapel—not God, but the god that is in the detail. He was led to the dubious extreme of aspiring to a Church vocation by the promise of momentary perfections he suspected he could know only in ritual—exaltations whereby, in his words, "the elements of our nature refine themselves to the burning point." To burn, he wrote in "Diaphaneite" (1864), his first surviving essay, is to will oneself into transparency, into crystal. It is to attain to the condition of art:

The artist and he who treats life in the spirit of art desires only to be shown to the world as he really is; as he comes nearer and nearer to perfection, the veil of an outer life not simply expressive of the inward becomes thinner and thinner. This intellectual throne is rarely won. Like the religious life, it is a paradox in the world, denying the first conditions of man's ordinary existence, cutting obliquely the spontaneous order of things.

Pater's work is invariably a search for denials of the first conditions of ordinary experience, a cutting of spontaneous orders by the oblique strategies of his artifice: as the sacred rebuts the profane, so he intends his sentences to dispel the ordinary. Accordingly, from the outset of his career he fastens onto the liturgy as prototype of the artistic act. For what he finds in priestly gestures is a purging away of all that is not form. It is just this sense of the sacerdotal as purification that leads him to place it first among his tropes. Burning with a hard gemlike flame means for Pater the dissolution of ordinary experience into hieratic clarity, into art.

But is the ritual of refinement he will enact in the essays and "imaginary portraits" a case of burning always with hard, gemlike flame? Is it not, more modestly, a matter of keeping the self awake and ready to answer experience, of taking care of the self? "For all Pater says about passion, eagerness, and excitement," says Graham Hough, "intensity of experience is not really what he is after; . . . whatever it may be to burn with a hard gem-like flame, it is something that takes place at a rather low temperature."[1] Wittingly or not, Hough

echoes a remark Henry James had made in a letter to Edmund
Gosse a few months after Pater's death:

He reminds me, in the disturbed midnight of our actual literature,
of one of those lucent matchboxes which you can place, on going to
bed, near the candle, to show you in the darkness, where you can
strike a light: he shines in the uneasy gloom—vaguely, and has a
phosphorescence, not a flame.

What is of permanent value in Pater, I want to argue, is
the extraordinary demand made on writing itself. Out of his
certainty that words alone are certain good comes a new
kind of fortitude, countering hopes for sublimity with the
acknowledgment that a mere phosphorescence, this side of
the sublime, is all of ecstasy we shall get. Pater is always
trying to write his way out of phosphorescence and into
flame. But the release is checked again and again; what he
achieves is at best a momentary semblance of being set free.
Pater's performance does not set the self on fire; it struggles,
far more modestly, to keep the self from winking out altogether. He cannot rely on meditative recollection, years that
bring the philosophic mind, as a source of ballast and equa-
nimity. At every turn in his work the self is thrown back on
the bare resources of mere writing; is, in other words, never
more in any written instant than words make of it. Pater's
pen cuts "obliquely the spontaneous order of things" in order
to attempt a new order, one that can accommodate the
writer's will. James gets at just this when he says of him,

I think he has had—will have had—the most exquisite literary
fortune: i.e. to have taken it out all, wholly, exclusively, with the
pen (the style, the genius) and absolutely not at all with the person.
He is the mask without the face.

Because who he is always remains for Pater a matter of the
present tense—thus the emphatic argument of the Conclusion to his first book, *Studies in the History of the Renaissance* (1873)—he is in each writing moment obliged to shape

a further identity for the self. The program for living he lays down in the Conclusion translates into a program for writing, the imperative of being present to experience into that of being present to the perfecting shape words confer upon experience. The concerns of Pater as aesthete and as writer resolve into a single urgent question: "How shall we pass most swiftly from point to point and be present always at the focus where the greatest number of vital forces unite in their purest energy?"

In *Marius the Epicurean* (1885)—the prose romance he wrote as an apologia for the scandalizing Conclusion to his first book—Pater says of his young hero,

In a shadowy world, his deeper wisdom had ever been, with a sense of economy, with a jealous estimate of gain and loss, to use life, not as the means to some problematic end, but as far as might be, from dying hour to dying hour, as an end in itself—a kind of music, all-sufficing to the duly trained ear, even as it died out on the air.

And Pater's deeper wisdom is to use words as Marius uses life. "Not the fruit of experience," sings the Conclusion, "but experience itself is the end." Not the fruit of words—an ethic, or edification, or image of life—but words themselves are the end.

What I find in Pater's admittedly peculiar prose is something worth the trouble: a record of inevitably thwarted insights in a world where past is dead, future a conjecture, and the present a knife's edge.[2] It is in just this insistence on the pure present of life that Pater strikes us as so modern, reminds us more of our century than of his own. Like Wallace Stevens in his poems, Pater in his prose must continually find out with what wine and what bread to nourish "the empty spirit in vacant space." The burden thus to go on reinventing the self by means of words alone is typically caricatured and cheapened by a term like "aestheticism," fraught as it is with the connotations of depletion and retreat. Pater has more in common with Emerson than with Gautier or Whistler, shares with the Concord sage a costly conviction that "life only avails, not the having lived," that "power ceases in the instant of repose," that it is only within the narrow compass of the present that a self is won or lost.

And yet, the comparison holds only up to a point. For Pater's Romanticism is of the waning kind. He hasn't anything like the sublime Emersonian uncontainment. In the present of experience, where Emerson found an infinitude of himself, Pater will come only upon impassable boundaries.

He chooses prose as a medium in order to get at "the salt of poetry": those minimal certainties the unsparing exercise of the intellect leaves intact. "Why do you always write verse?" he'd asked Oscar Wilde when they first met. "Prose is so much more difficult." And Pater is seized early on by the fascination of what is difficult. It leads him simultaneously to abandon Christianity and verse making—for his faithlessness and his prose are related as obverse to reverse, and his literary production from "Diaphaneite" onward is a long ritual of unbelief. As for young Marius the Epicurean, so for young Walter Pater: "An exact estimate of realities, as towards himself, he must have—a delicately measured gradation of certainty in things—from the distant, haunted horizon of mere surmise or imagination, to the feeling of sorrow in his heart." But the refining that Marius, like his author, pursues leaves him with only "the sharp apex of the present moment between two hypothetical eternities." Pater's prose will continually reaffirm this "salt of poetry," this minimal certitude, besieging the narrow apex of the present for all it can be made to yield.

There is profound philosophical seriousness in him, a concerted epistemic inquiry that our term "aesthete" has mostly served to obscure. Only if we take the word etymologically can it show us Pater for who he was. The *aisthētēs*, in Greek, is one who sees. The modern aesthete is one who keeps faith with his seeing, for whom the unseen, the suprasensory, is a conceit at best, worked up from the flood of sense. The aesthetic man is bound, then, to be agnostic not only about God, but about everything that is higher—about truth, about the past, finally about the self:

That clear, perpetual outline of face and limb is but an image of ours, under which we grasp them—a design in a web, the actual threads of which pass out beyond it. This at least of flame-like our life has, that it is but the concurrence, renewed from moment to moment, of forces parting sooner or later on their ways.

These words put us less in mind of Lord Henry Wotton than of Heraclitus of Ephesus, whose most famous text—"All things give way; nothing abides"—Pater places at the head of his Conclusion to *The Renaissance*. Translated into the terms of modern skepticism, this means: "my self reduces without remainder to the fleeting present of my empirical experience." And there, for Pater, lies the hard truth—that experience is always and only mine, that the prisonhouse of sense, of subjectivity, is not to be evaded:

Experience, already reduced to a swarm of impressions, is ringed around for each one of us by that thick wall of personality through which no real voice has ever pierced on its way to us, or from us to that which we can only conjecture to be without. Every one of those impressions is the impression of the individual in his isolation, each mind keeping as a solitary prisoner its dreams of a world. Analysis goes a step further still, and assures us that those impressions of the individual mind to which, for each one of us, experience dwindles down, are in perpetual flight; that each of them is limited by time, and that time is infinitely divisible, also; all that is actual in it being a single moment, gone while we try to apprehend it, of which it may ever be more truly said that it has ceased to be than that it is. To such a tremulous wisp constantly reforming itself on the stream, to a single sharp impression, with a sense in it, a relic more or less fleeting, of such moments gone by, what is real in our life fines itself down. It is with this movement, with the passage and dissolution of impressions, images, sensations, that analysis leaves off—that continual vanishing away, that strange, perpetual weaving and unweaving of ourselves.

Passages, dissolutions, vanishings—and an irremediable aloneness as the condition of our receptivity. Thus the fined-down reality wherein "after all we must needs make the most of things."[3] Failure here will be *loneliness*, the impotence of the self to find a sufficiency in its own opportunities—the incapacity for *solitude*. For that and no mere intensity is Pater's grail. He writes against a ceaseless threat of loneliness, of failure to be "present at the focus." As he had said early on, "The demand of the intellect is to feel itself alive." It is in the redemptiveness of solitude and nowhere else that this demand can be met, for loneliness is Pater's death-in-life or absence from a longed-for strong self. The profane ritual he performs in words is an attempt to transubstantiate loneliness into solitude, absence into presence, death into life.

This craving for deliverance, as salient in the criticism as in the fiction, suggests the unbeliever who wishes he were not one. Hankering after something, anything, to put in the place where God had been, Pater finds *genius*, and this is always his real subject when he considers literature or art. His focus is not on the works themselves but on the "strange souls" to whom we owe them. Moreover, what seems his impulse to revere genius hides a deeper impulse to be at one with it, to enjoy the master's solitude as his own. To be absent from the focus is to be lonely; to be present there, identified with genius, is to have achieved the self-sufficiency of solitude, of presence. Encounters between Paterian loneliness and Paterian solitude register in his criticism as the conflict between two irreconcilable forms of sensibility: on the one hand, a conventionally cultured love of the old things genius has wrought and, on the other, a visionary and competitive wish to cancel out all distances between old and new, between the earliness of genius and the subsequence of mere appreciation.

Jakob Burckhardt, the great historian of Renaissance Italy,

located the psychic sources of the appreciative or cultivated attitude in "our unfulfilled yearning for that which has vanished"—*unsere unerfullte Sehnsucht nach dem Untergegangenen.*[4] Pater would certainly recognize his own longings in that formula. But unlike Burckhardt, Pater cannot make do with the ordinary gestures of learned retrospect. Instead he is driven on beyond the traditional sense of the past toward the chance for a visionary success over time's disjunctions. His will to the unmediated possession of and identification with certain vanished personalities is steady and concerted, the leading force in his criticism. He would breathe life into a master who is his own and himself through enabling exertions of style, the way things get turned.

"The term is right," he says, "and has its essential beauty, when it becomes, in a manner, what it signifies." Writing acquires for Pater a sacramental sense inasmuch as he wills by style alone to work the needful change of now for then. As a critic his aim was identification with his subjects, the commingling of his own blood with the blood of genius. Having relinquished a youthful taste for the High Church sacraments, the mature writer conceived for himself an ulterior eucharist—overestimating the power of his own (or any) enactment of style, proposing his sentences themselves as the crucible whereby the longed-for passage into presence may take place, and aloneness be experienced as sufficiency. Pater's criticism is an effort continually to draw the self forth from its lonely confinement and to deliver it into identity, through strength of felt poise and radiance, with one or another of the strange souls—Coleridge, Wordsworth, or Lamb; Winckelmann, Leonardo, Botticelli, Pico, or Michelangelo— to whom he has confided sublime and uncompromising hopes. Imagined weddings of their flesh and blood to his own put him in possession neither of knowledge nor of redemption but of fugitive sufficiencies that signify a passing, fancied perfection of the self, "gone while we try to apprehend

it, of which it may ever be more truly said that it has ceased
to be than that it is."

Lord Clark—by way of Bernard Berenson a spiritual grandson to Pater—believed the second prose romance, *Gaston de
Latour*, would have been still better than *Marius* had Pater
completed it.[5] Unfortunately, we have only the five chapters
which appeared serially in *Macmillan's Magazine* in 1888,
plus three further sequences (one of which remains unpublished). It is odd that this torso should have been ignored by
most of Pater's critics, for it reveals his philosophical enterprise with particular candor. In a chapter called "Suspended
Judgement"—an evocation of Montaigne that deserves to
rank with Emerson's great essay—Gaston comes for what
turns into a stay of nine months at the Sieur's tower. Montaigne is thirty-six, our hero little more than a youth. The
older man, his great book still ahead of him, puts before the
younger what will become the fundamental avowal of the
Essais: the self as not less than a vocation, a daily labor and
lifework of subjective inspection. "I have no other end in
writing," Montaigne will insist, "but to discover myself."
"And what," asks Pater,

was the purport, what the justification of this undissembled ego-
tism? It was the recognition, over against, or in continuation of,
that world of floating doubt, of the individual mind, as for each
one severally, at once the unique organ, and the only matter, of
knowledge,—the wonderful energy, the reality and authority of
that, in its absolute loneliness, conforming all things to its law,
without witnesses as without judge, without appeal, save to itself.
Whatever truth there might be, must come for each one from
within, not from without. . . . One's own experience!—that, at
least, *was* one's own: low and earthly, it might be; still, the earth
was, emphatically, good, good-natured; and he loved, emphatically,
to recommend the wisdom, amid all doubts, of keeping close to it.

The wisdom of keeping close to earth is another version
of the aesthetic credo, another way of keeping faith with

appearances, the realm of things that come to be and pass away. But, crucially, what Pater has found in the "absolute loneliness" of Montaignian self-reflexivity is no break with but a continuation of the flux or "world of floating doubt." The aesthetic man, keeper of faith with appearances, has no exonerated substance of his own to set over against the mutability of things. In the Heraclitean first chapter of *Plato and Platonism* (1893) Pater will write that "the principle of lapse, of waste" is in ourselves and not just the world we confront, and that we are thus implicated without remainder in those "masterful currents of universal change, stealthily withdrawing the apparently solid earth itself from beneath one's feet." The self is nothing more for Pater than what it has power at any given moment to attend to and admire; and what it attends to and admires cannot but vanish. Here no one and nothing enjoys metaphysical exemption. The only truth about the self and the world is their transit. (Such is the notion of truth that Emerson, himself acknowledging Montaigne as predecessor, claimed to write in loyalty to: "It is the peculiarity of Truth that it must live every moment in the beginning, in the middle, and onward forever in every stage of statement. I cannot accept without qualification the most indisputable of your axioms. I see that they are not quite true."[6])

Truth as becoming. Appearance as the only reality. The mask without the face. This repudiation of the metaphysical forms one powerful current in Pater's work. But it is only half the story. As his cultivated pieties are crossed in the criticism by a visionary hankering to be identified with, not simply to admire, the earliness of genius, so his will to immanence is crossed in the fiction by a countervailing will to transcendence. What he calls in *Gaston* "those problematic heavenly lights that might find their way to one from infinite skies" do find their way resistlessly to him, and nowhere more beautifully than in the first and most autobiographical of his imaginary portraits, "The Child in the House" (1878) with its rendering of Florian Deleal, a boy simultaneously in love with the profane and the sacred:

A constant substitution of the typical for the actual took place in his thoughts. Angels might be met by the way, under the English elm or beech tree; mere messengers seemed like angels, bound on celestial errands; a deep mysticity brooded over real meetings and partings; marriages were made in heaven; and deaths also, with hands of angels thereupon, to bear soul and body quietly asunder, each to its appointed rest. All the acts and accidents of daily life borrowed a sacred colour and significance; the very colours of things became themselves weighty with meanings like the sacred stuffs of Moses' tabernacle, full of penitence or peace. Sentiment, congruous in the first instance only with those divine transactions, the deep effusive unction of the House of Bethany, was assumed as the due attitude for the reception of our every-day existence; and for a time he walked through the world in a sustained, not unpleasurable awe, generated by the habitual recognition, beside every circumstance and event of life, of its celestial correspondent.

But the child in the house learns, as do all of Pater's auto-biographical heroes, that the beauties of the earth are covenanted with death. And a death that does not turn back into life. Hence Gaston de Latour's dismay of an Easter Sunday:

The sudden gaieties of Easter morning, the congratulations to the Divine Mother, the sharpness of the recoil from one extreme of feeling to another, for him never cleared away the Lenten pre-occupation with Christ's death and passion; the empty tomb, with the white clothes lying, was still a tomb; there was no human warmth in the "spiritual body": the white flowers, after all, were those of a funeral, with a mortal coldness, amid the loud Alleluias, which refused to melt at the startling summons, any more than the earth will do in the March morning because we call it Spring.

But Gaston is of two inclinations, and where Easter Mass fails him the feast of the Pentecost does not:

It was altogether different with the other festival which celebrates the Descent of the Spirit, the tongues, the nameless impulses gone all abroad, to soften, to penetrate, all things, as with the winning subtlety of nature, or of human genius. The gracious Pentecostal fire seemed to be in alliance with the sweet, warm, relaxing winds of that later, securer, season, bringing their spicy burden from unseen sources. Into the close world, like a walled garden, about him, influences from remotest time and space found their way, traveling unerringly on their long journeys, as if straight to him, with the assurance that things were not wholly left to themselves.

This, I think, unveils the essential cross-play in Pater. Florian Deleal's "misgivings as to the ultimate tendency of the years" register in all the books as a baffled turning to and from the larger hope. It is the dream of an adamant of Being, some inviolable assurance that things are not left wholly to themselves, which again and again breaks in on the Paterian celebration of the universe of phenomena, exposing it as a universe of death.

"As soon as we imagine someone," Nietzsche writes in a note of 1887, "who is responsible for our being thus and thus, etc. (God, nature), and therefore attribute to him the intention that we should exist and be happy or wretched, we corrupt for ourselves the *innocence of becoming*. We then have someone who wants to achieve through us and with us."[7] Compare Walter Pater, who could never really get rid of metaphysical need, never really embrace the flux, never like Nietzsche hail the innocence of becoming. Pater's mutable universe shimmers with a treachery held in reserve. One thinks of that alluring basket of apples in "The Child in the House":

Coming in one afternoon in September, along the red gravel walk, to look for a basket of yellow crabapples left in the cool, old parlour, he remembered it the more, and how the colors struck upon him, because a wasp on the bitten apple stung him, and he felt the passion of sudden, severe pain.

Here is quintessential Pater, the promise of pleasure instinct with the promise of pain. Innocence of becoming is, for him, the goodly illusion, treachery of becoming the bitter fact.

Just before writing "The Child in the House" he had, in the original version of "The School of Giorgione," mused on our desire that the high occasions of experience not be fleeting:

Who, in some such perfect moment, when the harmony of things inward and outward beat itself out so truly, and with a sense of receptivity, as if in that deep accord, with entire inaction on our part, some messenger from the real soul of things must be on his way to one, has not felt the desire to perpetuate all that, just so, to suspend it in every particular circumstance, with the portrait of just that one spray of leaves lifted just so high against the sky above the well, forever?—a desire how bewildering with the question whether there be indeed any place wherein these desirable moments take permanent refuge.[8]

To ask about the place where moments take permanent refuge is to ask about forever. Pater is always trying to write his way out of loneliness and into solitude, out of the ordinariness of Pater and into the grandeur of genius—out of the world of floating doubt and into some abiding place, some permanence. His Montaigne counsels Gaston de Latour that doubt is the best of pillows to sleep on; but neither Gaston nor his author can make do with suspended judgment as a spiritual solution; their *Wissensdrang* or spiritual craving is for nothing less than the sublime.

What is that? The *Peri Hupsos* of Longinus, rediscovered in the seventeenth century, basic to eighteenth- and nineteenth-century thinking about poetics, adduces a natural greatness *(to megalophues)* of the mind, and defines the sublime *(to hupsos)* as an echo in words of that inward majesty—a certification of the infinite in us. "The whole universe," writes Longinus, "is not sufficient for the extensive reach and piercing speculation of the human understanding. It passes the bounds of the material world, and launches forth at pleasure into endless space." The greatest modern philosopher of the sublime, Kant, defines it in his *Critique of Judgment* as "that in comparison with which all else is small." And Thomas Weiskel, a recent expositor, similarly understands the sublime as an argument about our hidden kinship to what surpasses us without measure. "The essential claim of the sublime," Weiskel writes, "is that man can, in feeling and in speech, transcend the human."[9] What I want to stress in the present connection is that sublime *expectation*, the drive to transcendence, surfaces again and again in Pater, despite a willed commitment to becoming as the only truth. Whatever his apparent ideal of self-culture as a preparation for the fair moments of fleeting experience, Pater schooled himself more deeply for an eventual deliverance from the treachery of becoming, as here his hero in the culminating chapter of *Marius the Epicurean:*

Throughout the elaborate and lifelong education of his receptive powers, he had ever kept in view the purpose of preparing himself towards possible further revelation someday—towards some ampler vision, which would take up into itself and explain this world's delightful shows, as the scattered fragments of a poetry, til then but half understood, might be taken up into the text of a lost epic, recovered at last. At this moment, unclouded receptivity of soul, grown so steadily through all those years, from experience to experience, was at its height; the house ready for the possible guest, the tablet of the mind white and smooth, for whatsoever divine fingers might choose to write there.

The guest does not arrive, of course. Divine fingers inscribe no text. The loneliness of the self is not evaded. Receptivity does not become vision. Ignorance does not become knowledge. Hence, at the end of "The Poetry of Michelangelo," the old sculptor-painter-poet has managed to shore only hope and ignorance against his ruin:

What hope he has is based on the consciousness of ignorance—ignorance of man, ignorance of the nature of the mind, its origin and capacities. Michelangelo is so ignorant of the spiritual world, of the new body and its laws, that he does not surely know whether the consecrated host may not be the body of Christ. And of all that range of sentiment he is the poet, a poet still alive and in possession of our inmost thoughts—dumb inquiry over the relapse of death into the formlessness which preceded life, the change, the revolt from that change, then the correcting, hallowing, consoling rush of pity; at last, far off, thin and vague, yet no more vague than the most definite thoughts men have had through three centuries on a matter that has been so near their hearts, the new body—a passing light, a mere intangible, external effect, over those too rigid or too formless faces; a dream that lingers a moment, retreating into the dawn, incomplete, aimless, helpless; a thing with faint hearing, faint memory, faint power of touch; a breath, a flame in the doorway, a feather in the wind.

A revelation, in brief, that does not take place. Pater's Michelangelo cannot say whether the dream of the new body—of the triumph over death—is mocked by time. Poet of the longing that it not be so, this Michelangelo comes at last to Christian sureties only because not knowing has worn him out; under the shelter of belief he is "consoled and tranquilised, as a traveler might be, resting for one evening in a strange city, by its stately aspect and the sentiment of its many fortunes, just because with those fortunes he has nothing to do." His Christianity is, then, the façade behind which he goes on tending his doubt; like the other geniuses of *The Renaissance*, Pater's Michelangelo authenticates himself by all he cannot know.

More telling still is Pater's Leonardo, who never does—like his younger contemporary—succumb to the "sunless pleasures" of Christian observance. "Leonardo da Vinci" is Pater's first signed piece of work, first Renaissance study, and the centerpiece of his first book. Like Marius in the last clause of life, the dying Leonardo of Pater's imagination looks "forward to the vague land" and experiences "the last curiosity." But unlike his Michelangelo, his Leonardo gains no rest from the rigors of not knowing; in all of Pater's work he remains the leading hero of unbelief. This most moving of the essays (written, as it happens, in the year our word "agnostic" was first coined) bears a subtitle from Bacon, *Homo Minister et Interpres Naturae*—which means little until we read the entire aphorism in the *Novum Organum* from which it is drawn: "Man, as the minister and interpreter of nature, can do and understand only so much as he has observed, in fact or thought, of nature's order; beyond this he knows nothing and can do nothing." Here is the keynote to Pater's essay—Leonardo as the figure of metaphysical impotence and want. The first painter to have studied how nature works in order to represent her, who, as Michelet says, felt all of nature to be "as if his, loved by him,"[10] also experiences a great poverty in being confined to nature and having nothing beyond her to know and love. Leonardo expends his genius as if in the spell of some great melancholy, bound by the pattern of hesitation, indifference, disgust. *Dimmi semmai fu fatto chose,* he scribbles over and over into the margins of his notebooks—"Tell me if anything ever was done."[11] Turned resolutely to a world that is all that is the case, his eye—"whether in sorrow or scorn"— cannot help deriding that world: "Legions of grotesques sweep under his hand; for has not nature too her grotesques—the rent rock, the distorting lights of evening on lonely roads, the unveiled structure of man in the embryo, or the skeleton?"

Pater's Leonardo is an artist gifted for what Flaubert called "the bitter undertaste in everything." "Because I always sense the future," the latter had written to Louise Colet, "the antithesis of everything is always before my eyes. I have never seen a child without thinking it would grow old, nor a cradle without thinking of a grave. The sight of a naked woman makes me imagine her skeleton." Pater profoundly admired Flaubert and would in 1889 review a volume of the letters to "Madame X," as Louise was then known, letters identifying better than anything else I know what Pater is after in his Leonardo essay: a sensibility not only adding strangeness to beauty (this will be his formula for Romanticism), but insisting on a variety of strangeness that shades— suavely, implacably—into the grotesque.

His choice of Leonardo as subject was surely a response to Ruskin, who had written earlier that same year in *The Queen of the Air* that da Vinci "depraved his finer instincts by caricature, and remained to the end of his days the slave of an archaic smile." Standing up to this meant refuting the greatest authority on the visual arts to have written in England before or since, and Pater, a man of intellectual daring but personal reserve, was not one for the direct assault. Yet as the embodiment of an untrammeled curiosity wedded to the desire for beauty, his Leonardo represents the obsolescence of the sacred and the full claim of modernity—all that Ruskin most abhorred. In the beauty of the Gioconda, for example, Pater finds the whole religious gamut of Europe, pagan as well as Christian, but sicklied over by our estranging secularism, our distance from those numinous sources of power and feeling. His Mona Lisa embodies

the animalism of Greece, the lust of Rome, the mysticism of the middle age with its spiritual ambition and the imaginative loves, the return of the Pagan world, the sins of the Borgias. She is older than the rocks among which she sits; like the vampire she has been dead many times, and learned the secrets of the grave; and has been a diver in deep seas, and keeps their fallen day about her; and traffiked for strange webs with Eastern merchants, and, as Leda, was the mother of Helen of Troy and, as Saint Anne, the mother of Mary; and all this has been to her as but the sound of lyres and flutes, and lives only in the delicacy with which it has moulded the changing lineaments, and tinged the eyelids and the hands. The fancy of a perpetual life, sweeping together ten thousand experiences, is an old one; and modern philosophy has conceived the idea of humanity as wrought upon by, and summing up in itself, all modes of thought and life. Certainly Lady Lisa might stand as the embodiment of the old fancy, the symbol of the modern idea.

Most of Pater's critics have attempted to interpret this very famous passage, but only Harold Bloom has made real inroads, I think, identifying the lady both with the unredemptive universe of becoming *and* with the intimated promise of a triumph over time. "Pater dreads and desires her," Bloom writes,

or perhaps desires her precisely through his dread. . . . The Lady Lisa, as an inevitable object for the quest for all which we have lost, is herself a process moving towards a final entropy, summing up all the estrangements we have suffered. . . . She incarnates too much, both for her own good and for ours. The cycles of civilization, the burden our consciousness bears, render us latecomers, but the Lady Lisa perpetually carries the seal of a terrible priority.[12]

The overdetermined lady balances enticement and dismissal in her level gaze. Embodying too much, she seems simultaneously to minister to and ridicule us in our incomprehension, refusing either to dispel or affirm the larger hope. She grants only that things may or may not be what they seem in a world wound down and desacralized.

Now to her neighbor in the Louvre, *St. John the Baptist*, "whose delicate brown flesh," Pater writes, "no one would go out into the desert to seek, and whose treacherous smile would have us understand something far beyond the outward gesture or circumstance." What he finds in the Baptist is a pagan deity in Christian disguise, one of Heine's gods in exile who catch as catch can in a world that has renounced them. A finger points heavenward, true, but this Saint John—really a Bacchus in disguise—seems only to taunt us with the prospect of eternity. "He points to heaven," Gautier had written in an essay of 1864 that Pater knew, "but he derides it, and seems to laugh at the credulity of the spectators."[13] A year later Hippolyte Taine would find in Leonardo's Baptist the archtrope of spiritual perversity. But it was Michelet who, earliest, had looked deepest and given Pater his best lead, pronouncing the Baptist and all of Leonardo's figures in the Louvre "gods, but sick gods,"[14] forced from their high seats into anonymity when, as Heine puts it, "the true lord of the world planted his crusading banner on the castle of heaven."[15]

Constrained to a life out of due time, Denys l'Auxerrois of the story by that name and Apollyon of "Apollo in Picardy"—Pater's two overt versions in the imaginary portraits of pagan divinity in Christian exile—stand for an amplitude of existence that Christianity has everywhere run to earth. Like Renan, whom he had read, like Nietzsche, whom he almost certainly had not, Pater regards the Greek pantheon as a transfiguring mirror: the all-too-human gazes back, rendered perfect, for what the archaic Greeks did was to fashion gods after their own image, divinizing existence itself rather than some essence beyond. "How else," asks Nietzsche in *The Birth of Tragedy*, published one year before *The Renaissance*, "could this people, so sensitive, so vehement, so singularly capable of *suffering*, have endured existence, if it had not been revealed to them in their gods, surrounded by a higher glory?"

Pater understands the difference between pagan and Christian deity very simply: the one proclaims the innocence, the other the guilt, of becoming. He sets forth in his first book, as does Nietzsche in his, a "Hellenic ideal, in which man is at unity with himself, with his physical nature, with the outward world." The more we contemplate it, he writes, "the more we may be inclined to regret that he should ever have passed beyond it, to contend for a perfection that makes the blood turbid, and frets the flesh, and discredits the actual world about us." Pater posits a Greece in which life itself suffices, is the end of life. For him, the heart of Greek paganism is the plenary Yes it says to earth. In this connection, it may be recalled that he places at the front of *The Renaissance* a biblical motto: "Yet shall ye be as the wings of a dove." The whole passage in the Book of Psalms runs, "Though ye have lain among the pots, yet shall ye be as the wings of a dove covered with silver, and her feathers with yellow gold." It is just this longing for deliverance that Pater's and Nietzsche's early Greeks do not feel. Mortal in their expectation, they lie without regret among the potsherds of becoming.

The Renaissance is notoriously a book with an argument. Everywhere in its rhetoric is the chant of life itself as the end of life:

While all melts under our feet, we may well grasp at any exquisite passion, or any contribution to knowledge that seems by a lifted horizon to set the spirit free for a moment, or any stirring of the senses, strange dyes, strange colors, curious odours, or work of the artist's hands or the face of one's friend. Not to discriminate every moment some passionate attitude in those about us, and in the very brilliancy of their gifts some tragic dividing of forces on their ways, is, on this short day of frost and sun, to sleep before evening.

Here is the unmistakable current by which we know Pater. But tread this prose more deeply and you cannot but feel the undertow. His Renaissance is an outbreak of pagan sentiment within the renunciatory context of medieval life: "the older gods had rehabilitated themselves," he writes in the essay on Pico, "and men's allegiance was divided." Accordingly, art begins the turn from mystical to sensuous aims, to "the life of the senses and the blood—blood no longer dropping from the hands in sacrifice, as with Angelico, but as with Titian, burning in the face for desire and love."[16] Man unlearns "the crucifixion of these senses"[17] and trains himself instead to a responsiveness "making the earth golden and the grape fiery for him." A new aesthetic culture defies the old ascetic claims:

The spiritualist is satisfied as he watches the escape of the sensuous elements from his conceptions; his interest grows, as the dyed garment bleaches in the keener air. But the artist steeps his thought again and again into the fire of color. To the Greek this immersion in the sensuous was religiously indifferent. Greek sensuousness, therefore, does not fever the conscience: it is shameless and child-like. Christian asceticism, on the other hand, discrediting the slightest touch of sense, has from time to time provoked into strong emphasis the contrast or antagonism to itself, of the artistic life, with its inevitable sensuousness.

But Pater is not content, like conventional aesthetes from Gautier onward, merely to worship at the altar of strangeness added to beauty. He is also intent on reckoning the cost. Like the figures of his Botticelli—"always attractive, clothed sometimes by passion with a character of loveliness and energy, but saddened perpetually by the shadow upon them of the great things from which they shrink"—Pater's aestheticism is a troubled and sorrowful repudiation of ultimate concern, a *gran rifiuto* that counts the wages of abstention and is not cheered. Like Botticelli's madonnas, Pater is "one of those who are neither for Jehovah nor for his enemies," and this retracted neutrality is for him the little proving ground of art, "in which men take no side in great conflicts, and decide no great causes." This art of the "middle world" is for its own sake and not, like Dante's, for a Love that moves the sun and the other stars.

Pater accepts unflinchingly that death has set its seal on the beautiful. Such is his only stable assurance in the world of floating doubt, imparting an infernal resonance to those pure avowals of art that are, for him, testimony to our loss of an absolute criterion. Art for its own sake has already become in Pater's first book—albeit very quietly—what it will be for the mature Nietzsche: "the virtuoso croakings of shivering frogs, despairing in their swamp."[18] Radical weddings of beauty to becoming consign Pater to what conventional aesthetes from Gautier to the nineties mistook for paradise, but which Pater, like Hermann Broch a half-century later, knows to be "the hells of *l'art pour l'art*."[19]

And indeed, in *The Renaissance,* a book about the historical moment when art (at least according to Pater) slips its theological moorings, each of the great ones has, in virtue of his singular estrangement from God, an inferno all his own. Here is Pico, who lies "down to rest in the Dominican habit, yet amid thoughts of the older gods"; here du Bellay, consoled only by his sentiment of *la grandeur du rien*; here Winckelmann, the "born heathen" (as Goethe called him) who makes a show of converting to Catholicism as the price of his passage to Rome, but arrives with the works of Voltaire scandalously in his possession. And here, of course, stands "the profanest of painters," master of the *Cenacolo* at Santa Maria delle Grazie, whose Christ sits among a company of ghosts as "faint as the shadows of the leaves upon the wall on autumn afternoons." Pater clearly prefers the *Last Supper* in its blighted sorry state, chooses to find there Leonardo's original intent. For he sees that time has folded into a single party the eleven bound, by tradition, for the highest heaven and the one bound, by tradition, for the deepest hell. These twelve belong neither to God nor to his enemies. They belong instead to time, which has made shadows of them, as time will. And "this figure," writes Pater of the thirteenth, the man at the center, "is but the faintest, the most spectral of them all."

When a student brought home word to his parents that the author of *The Renaissance* had one day pronounced faith "a loathsome disease," the boy's father dispatched a letter taking Pater to task. Pater answered with doubts that he would have used a word like "loathsome" and suggested that faith might more accurately be called "a *beautiful* disease." And what, you wonder, did the boy's father say to that?

Walter Pater's spiritual place lies somewhere between the beautiful disease and what Nietzsche called the great health. I am arguing that this in-betweenness is what Pater is writing against, that he is in search of a deliverance from the habitual vagaries. His direction is out of coming-to-be and into the ultimate. But always the ecstatic movement is thwarted and Pater returned to an abiding rhetorical loneliness. He does not even begin to discern his way into the solitude of Zarathustra's Yes and Amen. Repudiating the way back to orthodoxy, he does not thereby gain the way forward to an earthly absolute. He is left alone with time—which is to say he's left lonely, unable to cry with the Nietzschean hero, "I love you, O eternity!" and thereby mean only becoming and destruction exalted into the godhead of an eternal recurrence. Pater's eucharist cannot expiate the guilt of becoming. Words remain words. Time remains time. Death remains death.

And so it must be, for the one god Pater knows is mutation. As for his master Heraclitus, so for him: the one is the many. The Ephesian later antiquity called "the weeping philosopher"—first to collapse the metaphysical into time, Being into becoming, the one into manyness—finds only in turnings of fire upon itself a suitable trope of the real: "The ordering, the same for all, no god nor man has made, but it ever was and is and will be: fire everliving, kindled in measures and in measures going out."[20] Heraclitean deity *is* this fire, a chaos of coming-to-be, a manyness that admits of no reference to an origin: "The god: day and night, winter and summer, war and peace, satiety and hunger." With the collapse of the metaphysical into sheer becoming, the logic of identity collapses too. Things are not only what they are but also what they are not, for thinghood itself is a fiction; pure becoming is the pure chaos in which opposites embrace and the very basis for an intelligibility of things is undermined.

Yet Heraclitus, ancient father of our modern unbelief, perhaps saw his way clear to a kind of providence identical with random chaos: "Lifetime is a child at play," he says, "moving pieces in a game. Kingship belongs to the child." This is the strange argument for a world in which simultaneously nothing and everything is left to itself. The unsearchable moves of the child playing can equally well be glossed as cosmos or chaos, which may be what Heraclitus means when he writes, "The fairest order in the world is a heap of ran-

dom sweepings." The Heraclitean child playing, like the
Nietzschean eternal recurrence, signifies a total assimilation
of transcendence to immanence, providence to chance, eternity to time, meaning to meaninglessness.

Pater, of course, does not get so far. What became for Heraclitus one and the same remains for him an alternative; thus
he can but shuttle between two poles, neither of which satis-
fies him. The best critical summation of Pater may still be
Sidney Colvin's review of *The Renaissance* where he praises
"a philosophy which accepts objects as relative, experience as
everything, the Absolute as a dream—life as a flux, and consciousness as an incident in the encounter of forces."[21] If Pater calls "flux" what Nietzsche more aggressively terms
"chaos," he is as surely declaring an absence of intrinsic
meaning, of a thing-in-itself beyond the play of appearances.
The shapes and identities and substances we discern in the
world are, for Pater as for Nietzsche, human additions made
in accordance with human need. As the latter says, "The total
character of the world . . . is in all eternity chaos—in the
sense not of a lack of necessity but of a lack of order, arrange-
ment, form, beauty, wisdom, and whatever other names there
are for our aesthetic anthropomorphisms."[22]

Yet what we nowhere find in Pater is the sheer destructive
ebullience of Nietzsche's enterprise. Pater understands that
designating the total character of the world as flux means the
death of one and all gods. He understands, moreover, that the
death of one and all gods means the death also of the subject,
of substantial human identity; consciousness is thus, as they
say, decentered, demoted to the status of "an incident in the
encounter of forces." Like Nietzsche, Pater grasps all of this,
but unlike Nietzsche he grasps it unwillingly and with a
sense of dereliction:

Such thoughts seem desolate . . . at times all the bitterness of life
seems concentrated in them. They bring the image of one washed
out beyond the bar in a sea at ebb, losing even his personality, as
the elements of which he is composed pass into new combinations.

Struggling, as he must, to save himself, it is himself that he loses at every moment.[23]

Pater's inmost need is for the perished realm of origins that could give substantial identity to the subject, resolve the chaos of sheer consciousness into the stable contours of the individual, liberate selfhood from its wasting context.

Everywhere, to that end, he is riveted to issues of personality. These are the burden, formulated in his preface to *The Renaissance*, of the "aesthetic critic," as Pater liked to style himself:

In all ages there have been some excellent workmen, and some excellent work done. The question [the aesthetic critic] asks is always:—In whom did the stir, the genius, the sentiment of the period find itself? Where was the receptacle of its refinement, its elevation, its taste?

What genius signifies for Pater is personality at its highest attainment, a revelation out of the welter, a disclosure of meaning within the governing context of meaninglessness. These radiances, these great ones redeeming the waste of history, remind us of epiphanies of experience that in Pater stand forth from the waste of sensation:

A sudden light transfigures some trivial thing, a weathervane, a windmill, a winnowing-fan, the dust in the barn door. A moment— and the thing has vanished, because it was pure effect; but it leaves a relish behind it, a longing that the accident may happen again.

As the intense and isolated moment is related to what stretches before and after, so the sublimity of genius to our common days, belying chaos only to be belied in its turn. We cannot help finding in the evidence of genius an intimation of order in the world, for all that we acknowledge the master an accident, part and parcel of the flux.

Pater is in the end as agnostic about genius as he is about God, its prototype. But agnosticism, so often an uninteresting stance, has in his version a baffled dignity that moves us.

Avowing only a pure mutability at the heart of things, he is stricken by the absence of inherent meaning. Yet he relies on that same mutability as his sole resource for everything beautiful. And the occasions of beauty imply always for him the shade of a presentiment—here and gone—that things are not left wholly to themselves.

His philosophical father had declared that no man steps twice into the same river. And Cratylus went still further, claiming that no man steps in even once, for no man possesses even that much substantial being. Nietzsche, profoundest of Cratyleans, writes in the notebooks from his climactic phase,

The "subject" is not something given, it is something added and invented and projected behind what there is. . . . "The subject": interpreted from within ourselves, so that the ego counts as a substance, as the cause of all deeds, as a doer.

The logical-metaphysical postulates, the belief in substance, accident, attribute, etc., derive their convincing force from our habit of regarding all our deeds as consequences of our will—so that the ego, as substance, does not vanish in the multiplicity of change.— But there is no such thing as will.[24]

Something like Nietzsche's "continual transitoriness and fleetingness of the subject" is Pater's own theme. He knows with Nietzsche that even the last stronghold of meaning, the personal will, is a fiction, a mask superinduced like the others on chaos in order to stabilize and grant identity to what is only a perpetual weaving and unweaving.

Finally, Pater understands this: for the world to have meanings, the world must have a Meaning. He waits upon that Meaning, beguiling his time with the provisional putting of meanings into the world. In other words, he makes literature. But always in the knowledge that meanings ravel, that literature is a procedure undertaken against the inherent meaninglessness that must again and again prevail—in default, that is, of a Meaning.

Chapter 2

Paul Valéry,
or the Unmixed Cup

Narcissus bends to what is not. *Penche-toi. . . . Baise-toi. Tremble de tout ton être.*[1] Kneeling before his reflection in a pool, he dreams of the ultimate exclusion. Scorning nymphs to lust after a semblance of himself, Narcissus would abolish the claims of otherness. "My thirst," he declares, "is for the unmixed cup"[2]—selfhood, that is, without the admixture of a world. "I am my own drink."[3] Beauty beholding only itself, thought thinking itself alone:

> . . . moi, Narcisse aimé, je ne suis curieux
> Que de ma seule essence;
> Tout autre n'a pour moi qu'un coeur mystérieux.
> Tout autre n'est qu'absence.[4]

But when he leans out for the final consummation, Narcissus finds only distance, minute but unbesiegable:

> Je suis si près de toi que je pourrais te boire,
> Ô visage. . . . Ma soif est un esclave nu. . . .[5]

Self-knowledge—hovering there, intimately near. But unreal, a semblance only. How you gleam at last, pure goal of my striving!

> . . . . Et bientôt, je briserais, baiser,
> Ce peu qui nous défend de l'extrême existence,
> Cette tremblante, frêle, et pieuse distance

Entre moi-même et l'onde, et mon âme, et les
dieux! ...[6]

What the poems of Paul Valéry press toward is an always
receding promise of the pure. Comprised of deferrals, they
make of *expectancy* the essential poetic state of mind. For
the goal of the poem is, as he writes, "a frontier of the world;
one may not settle there."[7] Language is promiscuous. The
work of the poet is to reclaim for language a putative chas-
tity. Poems, says Valéry, "create an artificial and ideal order
by means of material of vulgar origin."[8] But the poetic impulse is, in fact, utopian. "Nothing so pure can coexist with
the circumstances of life." Poetry seeks to recover for words
a virtue that they never in the first instance had. For no poem
can just *be*, self-enfolded, absolute in its refusals; it is also
bound to *mean*. And meaning is tincture, fallenness, implication in the world.

A major perplexity tracks all of Valéry's work, poetry and
prose alike. It is that the purifying projects of thought he
gives his energies to are bound always to remain stigmatized
by a *worldliness* they profess to outbid, by what he calls "the
whole complex of incidents, demands, compulsions, solicitations of every kind and degree of urgency, which overtake
the mind without offering it any inner illumination, move it
only to disturb, and shift it away from the more important
toward the less."[9] Thinking remains, for him, contaminated
from the outset by its circumstances: a process of purification, yes, but one that never really cleanses, vexed as it is in
consequence of what Valéry calls the original "injustice"—
the fall into time and contingency that has engendered us as
natural beings, beholden to a world not of our design or
preference. Accordingly, the enactments of mind he prizes
most are always denaturing movements away from this ordinary psyche—consciousness as given—and toward the unat-
tainable marvel he calls "cogito" or consciousness as such.
As "pure poetry" remains for him an uninhabitable paradise

of words beyond the barrens of everyday language, so cogito beyond the wasteland of our habitual consciousness.

He liked to say of his master Mallarmé's work that it stood in relation to all previous poetry as algebra to arithmetic. Or as non-Euclidean geometries to traditional geometry. He credited Mallarmé with the most significant innovation in the history of words: an autotelic writing, absolute form seeking its own cause rather than discovering it in the experience of life. "He was unwilling to write," Valéry says, "without knowing what writing means and what that strange practice may signify."[10]

This demand for the fundamental implication of writing issued in a poetry too rich for anybody's blood, conceived as if the author had himself devised language from scratch. Mallarmé propounded the poem as a system of reciprocal resonances constituting an absolute, an inhuman discourse. "The subject," writes Valéry,

is no longer the *cause* of the form: it is one of its effects. Each line becomes an entity having physical reasons for existence. It is a discovery, a sort of "intrinsic truth" that has been wrenched from the domain of chance. As for the world, all reality has no other excuse for existence except to offer the poet the chance to play a sublime match against it—a match that is lost in advance.[11]

A notation from one of the last of Valéry's notebooks reads, "Poetry, for Mallarmé, was the essential and unique object. For me, a particular application of the mind's powers. This was the contrast."[12] Like his forebear, Valéry is an idolator. But whereas Mallarmé's idolatry waited upon a supposed Orphic power for overtaking the world in order to deliver it up to some terminal artifice—the Book, he liked to call it—Valéry subscribes to an ideal of pure consciousness by definition irreconcilable with any product or end result. He depreciates poems, paintings, edifices, philosophical systems, whatever sets a formal term to thinking, in favor of the hidden processes of thought which stand behind them. And while he does share Mallarmé's sense of a harassing disjunction between creative will and creative act, he is shielded from the sense of sterility that dogged Mallarmé, foredoomed literalist of the imagination, because he asks so much less of those shapes into which thought deposits itself. The poem, the painting, the edifice are always for him an *ébauche* or moment in the moving contour, never a finality or apotheosis of form.

Valéry in this way substitutes a utopia of the intelligence for the Mallarméan utopia of the Book. Propounding a supreme fiction of mental self-possession and power, he summons for himself a charmed identity to glister infinitely high above his own. Such is his profoundly skeptical account of genius. Out of "the real poverty" of worldliness, Valéry evokes the "imaginary wealth" of a utopian self.[13] Thus he again and again escapes despondence, attains in fact to comedy: by doubling consciousness as given into a fictive giant of itself, a *poésie pure* of the mind.

Dreams meant nothing to him. Mere sludge of sleep. The great thing was waking up. Toward dawn each day for more than half a century, Valéry would go to the notebooks in which he exactingly chronicled his consciousness. There he found renewal, as in "Aurore," the great opening poem of *Charmes* (1922):

> J'approche la transparence
> De l'invisible bassin
> Où nage mon Espérance
> Que l'eau porte par le sein.[14]

Mind is figured as the scene of a self-replenishing avidity. Thinking acquires the character of loving—it must be done again:

> Son col coupe le temps vague
> Et soulève cette vague
> Que fait un col sans pareil . . .

Elle sent sous l'onde unie
La profondeur infinie,
Et frémit depuis l'orteil.[15]

Limpid morning joys testify to the infinite recourse of thought. "Nothing is ever finished in the mind."[16] Here there is no ultimate grasping for heights or depths, only the renewed lateral reach of the intelligence. "The mind in itself," he writes, "has no means of setting a limit on its own fundamental activity, and there is no such thing as a thought which is its last thought."[17] Valéry is everywhere intent on this gladness of mental beginnings, the Intellectual Comedy, mind at its elated outset.

But repeatedly, helplessly, intellect is in default of itself. "Sometimes I think," he observes in the notebooks, "and sometimes I am."[18] For the thinker's life cannot be wholly a matter of thinking, any more than the dancer's can be wholly a matter of dance. To the axiom "It must be done again" we must add the corollary, "It must have a stop." I think this is the nerve of Valéry's dialogue "Dance and the Soul" (1921), in which Phaedrus, Eryximachus, and Socrates behold in motion "the astonishing and extreme dancer, Athikte." Socrates explains,

Just as in our minds hypotheses take shape symmetrically and possibles line up and are counted—so this body exercises itself in all its parts, joins in with itself, assumes shape upon shape, and goes out of itself incessantly![19]

It is as a continual burgeoning, not as the reach for truth, that Valéry understands consciousness. Its essence, like Athikte's, is to go out of itself. "She is a wave!" declares Phaedrus. "Do you not feel," asks Socrates, "that she is the pure act of metamorphosis?"[20] Her dance unfurls not what is but what is not—not "reality," but the unfailing exorbitance of the real. "Look at that body," says Socrates, "look how it spurns and betramples what is true! How it furiously, joyously destroys the very place upon which it is, and how it intoxicates itself with the excess of its changes."[21] For Valéry, mind is metamorphosis or it is nothing. "What are mortals for?" asks Eryximachus: "their business is to *know*. Know? And what is to know?—It is assuredly: not to be what one is."[22] Mind introduces into the deadly actualities a saving "leaven of what is not." Mind is the metamorphoses of the real.

So thinking is like dancing. And dancing is like love. "I cannot grow fond of anyone," Valéry writes, "without making him so vividly present to my mind that he becomes very different from himself."[23] And in another place: "I understand to the full what love might be. Excess of the real!"[24] Yet alongside the fabulous character of loving, he puts its self-frustration. Desire spends itself at the "impassable threshold,"[25] longing always for an I-know-not-what beyond. "Even as we demand of our soul many things for which it was not made," concludes the Socrates of "Dance and Soul,"

and require of it to illumine us, to prophesy, to divine the future, adjuring it even to discover the God—even so the body . . . wishes to attain to an entire possession of itself, and to a point of glory that is supernatural. . . . But our body fares as does the soul, for which the God and the wisdom, and the depth demanded of it are and can only be, moments, flashes, fragments of an alien time, desperate leaps out of its form.[26]

Thus dancing, thinking, loving emerge as Valéry's three types of the runaway who never gains his goal. He cannot, any more than Narcissus can consummate his self-love.

From this assertion of the similitude between Eros and thinking, a poetry of great power emerges. Its theme is the intermittences of mind, the way mind has of spending itself—the failure of mind at its inmost effort of self-possession. Valéry's poems are the chronicle of "that magnificent, eternal, crazy attempt *to see* that which *sees* and *express* that which *expresses*,"[27] an art of consciousness striving to bend back upon itself for its nourishment, "a poetry of the very

things of the mind."[28] Absurd by what it seeks, great by what
it finds, Valéryan consciousness gazes into the pool of itself
for culmination but comes upon poems instead, testimonies
to the impassable threshold:

> Comme le fruit se fond en jouissance,
> Comme en délice il change son absence
> Dans une bouche où sa forme se meurt,
> Je hume ici ma future fumée,
> Et le ciel chante à l'âme consumée
> Le changement des rives en rumeur.[29]

For Valéry, every poem is the site of a failure, as here in the
graveyard at Sète where he answers the glare of Mediterranean noon:

> Midi là-haut, Midi sans mouvement
> En soi se pense et convient à soi-même . . .
> Tête complète et parfait diadème,
> Je suis en toi le secret changement.[30]

The mind's desire is for finalities. But the fate of the mind is
to live without them, ever a pulse of change in what abides.
The refulgences of thinking are provisional, passing—like
lives. Consciousness remains an earthly fragment offered up
to the definitive radiance. Accordingly, "Le Cimetière
Marin" has as its symbol for the mind a necropolis.

Under the heading "Ex Nihilo" Valéry writes in his notebooks, "God made everything out of nothing. But the nothingness shows through."[31] At the cemetery by the sea, the
poet outfaces a world riddled with its own undoings, with
absence. "Allez!" cries consciousness. "Tout fuit! Ma présence est poreuse."[32] Consciousness stands its ground *entre le
vide et l'événement pur*[33]—between nullity and the fictive
apotheosis of mind or last thought.

French modernism began with Charles Baudelaire's unre-
alizable dream of attaining to "the new"—release from the
boring bitter round of sameness. For his poetic grandson

Valéry, by contrast, the new is all there ever is. Each moment is perforce the new, it being the nature of mind always to slough off the thought I momentarily am and make way for another, equally momentary, me. Heavy with his burden of regret, Baudelaire sought solace in a convulsive self-disclosure—*le coeur mis à nu.* For Valéry, on the other hand, nothing could be less to the point than a heart laid bare. "It must be rather fun," he writes, "by the mere fact of unbuttoning one's fly, to give oneself and other people the impression of discovering America. We all know perfectly well what we shall see, but at the first move everybody is excited."[34]

Baudelaire believed in sinfulness and unworthiness and saw each human self as if minted with these defects, conferring on it an identity not to be evaded. The indefeasibility of selfhood in Baudelaire is the indefeasibility of sin. To be sure, he propounds a magical *ailleurs* where all is pleasure—but stays moored fast to the sad actuality of his self-disgust. Nothing new for him, no means of escape, no grace; the infamy cannot be extirpated. Sinfulness gives the self something to be for a lifetime.

In Valéry there is nothing thus to tie up selfhood. The perdurable imposition of sin is replaced by the episodic grandeurs of thinking. Unmoored, we acknowledge an abyss opening to the right, but sail on by with a smile. For the wind is rising, and we must try to live—which for Valéry means being always elsewhere and other than where and what we are:

> . . . Debout! Dans l'ère successive!
> Brisez, mon corps, cette forme pensive!
> Buvez, mon sein, la naissance du vent!
> Une fraîcheur, de la mer exhalée,
> Me rend mon âme. . . . Ô puissance salée!
> Courons à l'onde en rejaillir vivant!
>
> Oui! Grande mer des délires douée
> Peau de panthère et chlamyde trouée

De mille et mille idoles du soleil,
Hydre absolue, ivre de ta chair bleue,
Qui te remords l'étincelante queue
Dans un tumulte au silence pareil. . . .[35]

His proverbial symbol of Necessity was the serpent, never more expressive than here in "Le Cimetière Marin" where it is the Mediterranean that writhes and coruscates, biting its tail in the gesture of an eternity at once tumultuous and mute. The device Valéry loved drawing best was a snake twined around a key. To the question his work everywhere puts in one form or another—*Que peut un homme?*—this colophon furnishes, I think, the emblematic response: reptilian caress of Necessity. A man can do something always, but never manage what is most fundamentally willed, never cut *les noeuds De l'eternelle halte*[36]—"the knots of the eternal cordon." If the mind need never feel stymied, neither may it ever feel wholly released. Paul Valéry is, by reputation, as pagan as they come. But it may be that his work secretes its own unwitting sense of sin. It may be that he is more profoundly the descendant of Baudelaire than we have imagined. Yes, the new is for Valéry all there is; but this ever-earliness turns out not to be the deliverance it seems. For the new intimates in each instant a recovered sense of what a man not only can but also cannot do.

He understood by "civilization" those energies that are unrelated to our survival. "For man's bread, clothing, and shelter, and his physical ills, neither Dante, nor Poussin, nor Malebranche could do anything whatever."[37] Civilizations have the fragility of lives, he liked to say. His remarkable political intelligence led him again and again, following the autumn of 1914, to question the outlook for a free and disinterested exercise of the mind. In 1925 he asks:

Can we be sure that bread, . . . that all the things essential to life may not one day be denied those men whose disappearance would in no way disturb the production of that bread and those things? The first to perish would be all those who cannot defend themselves by folding their arms. The rest would do likewise, or go back to practical work, overtaken by the rising poverty; and the progress of their extermination would, for some observer, demonstrate the actual hierarchy of the true needs of human life at its simplest.[38]

Fifteen years after he wrote these words, the Third Republic fell. Eulogizing Henri Bergson in the early months of German occupation, Valéry told his audience at the French Academy that they had buried more than just an old philosopher in the Jewish cemetery at Garches: "With each day that passes, civilization is further reduced to the memories and vestiges we keep of its multifarious riches and its free and abundant intellectual production.... Bergson seems already to belong to a past age and his name to be the last great name in the history of the European mind."[39] (This was splendid and brave, where and when it was uttered, and remarkable coming from one who had been anti-Dreyfusard in his youth.)

He felt, in that first year of Hitler's new European order, that the intelligence itself had come under occupation, and would be hounded to its death. "The abyss of history is deep enough to hold us all,"[40] he'd written years before. To the poetry of the very things of the mind, the longed-for Comedy of Intellect, history had given and would give its retort. In June of 1940 came the defeat of everything "Europe"—cherished word—had ever signified for Valéry. His response was *Mon Faust*, the fragmentary theater piece summing up, in a harsh minor key, many of the concerns that orient his career.[41] The titanism of Goethe's Faust, his eternal restless will to do and know, Valéry here replaces with a figure who, already when we meet him, has done and known all things. Mind as such, purified, absolved of its labors, Valéry's Faust constitutes in himself a first draft of that culminating book Mallarmé longed to achieve:

Well, I have this great work in mind. I want it to rid me finally of myself, of the self from which I already feel so detached. . . . I want to end up light, disburdened forever from anything . . . like a traveler who has thrown down his baggage and sets out at random, without a care for what he leaves behind.[42]

Valéry's Faust is at the end of his project—the terminal European, divested of the old humanistic will to accumulate and to master:

I am the present moment. . . . Nothing left over. No hidden depths. Infinity has become finite. What doesn't exist can no longer exist. If knowledge is what the mind must create, so that what IS may BE, I, FAUST, am become a pure and full knowledge. I am plenitude and consummation. I am he who I am. I am at the summit of my art.[43]

Faust has rid himself of his depths, attained to a consciousness that is mathematical in clarity and distinctness.

"I am tired of being Me! But that's saying very little— I'll say more! I am tired of being a Me—because that is to submit."[44] A late entry in the notebooks ascribes this indifferently to Faust or Monsieur Teste, the protagonist of Valéry's so-called novel of the same name. Both figures embody his utopian standard of genius—a protest against all forms of mind save the most fantastically pellucid; both "compensate the irregularity, the anisotropy of consciousness."[45] He understands a mind that unceasingly anatomizes its own processes as having escaped the defile of personality, of selfhood, the all-too-human. Edmond Teste is one such— Valéry's fictive absolute of thinking—the thinker clambering atop his own shoulders, jumping across his own shadow. He is the demon of pure possibility, an impossible thing, for Teste has got free of his conditions. He evades the Valéryan axiom that cognition may reign but cannot rule. In Teste cognition is absolute, released from the importunings of the hankering flesh and the historical world. What would have constituted a self, the feeling for the present tempered by past experience and future prospect, is replaced in Teste by the self-sufficient energies of thought thinking itself. An entry from the notebooks under the heading "Teste" reads,

Nothing is more humiliating than to feel suddenly that one is of one's own time, one's own country, that one has an origin, a name, a past, a bit of future; and above all, what a disgrace to feel regret, hope—that muck, that excrement befouling the best moment.[46]

Why the brief against personality? Because personalities are accidental rather than axiomatic. And is not genius, at least in Valéry's utopic version, immiscible with accidents or circumstances of any kind? Nothing so pure can coexist with life. He must regretfully own up to chance as the sum of man and to the inessential as our essence, rehearsed in anything we do or make. Acts of intellect bear perforce the compromising marks of selfhood. "There is no theory," he says, "that is not the fragment, carefully prepared, of some autobiography."[47] Persistently imagining a version of the mind detached from these circumstances, Valéry acknowledges a single heroism—that of the Self that outstrips selfhood. Teste is one such comic giant, Valéry's Descartes another. "What delights me in him," he writes of the first modern philosopher,

and makes him alive for me is his consciousness of himself—his whole being summoned to his own attention; a penetrating consciousness of the workings of his own thought; a consciousness so precise and so dominating that it transforms the Self into an instrument whose infallibility depends only on the degree of his consciousness of it.[48]

Descartes, as mythologized by Valéry, is a mind heroically disenthralled from otherness—the project of pure thought realized. Self thereby evades being a bundle of accidents and conditions, attains to *l'extrême hauteur*[49] of "I think." The Cartesian method of doubt is for Valéry a successful summoning of the whole mind to its own powers of attention. This act makes of consciousness an infallible instrument.

"There is only one thing to be done," he writes in the note-books, "and that is to remake oneself."[50] And yet, the one thing to be done cannot be done, he tacitly concedes. A Self remade along his lines, a purebred *res cogitans*, would be logically prior to everything else, unpledged to otherness. Consciousness can enjoy no such priority. Consciousness is vowed to the world, fleshed, incarnate—*le dieu dans la chair égaré*[51]—and can claim no rank outside of or above its context. Who is Descartes? A hero of the mind's priority. But who is Descartes, really? A Brer Rabbit struggling to get loose of the world, his tar baby.

Valéry's signal trait is a doubleness in his conception of man: wretched because of what he is, great because of what he imagines himself to be. Real poverty, imaginary wealth. "I am simultaneously on the crest of the wave and in its trough, watching it tower above me,"[52] he writes in a note-book. In the chess game played between being and thinking, being is bound always to remain at least one move ahead, he allows. But the game is never finished, mind can always start again. Like the palm in his poem of that name, reaching up and down to show both the pull of heaven and the make-weight of earth, thought is a middle term between plenitude and nothingness, betokening both:

> Ce bel arbitre mobile
> Entre l'ombre et le soleil,
> Simule d'une sibylle
> La sagesse et le sommeil.
> Autour d'une même place
> L'ample palme ne se lasse
> Des appels ni des adieux.[53]

Valéry's quarrel with himself renovates the old and distinguished quarrel between philosophy and poetry. "Poetry is not thought; it is the divinization of the Voice,"[54] he writes. Poetry does not need to be thought, because it does not aim to be truth. Philosophy, by contrast, signifies a will—

inherently cutting across the intent of poetry—to complete
the task of knowledge; to articulate a universe in words that
exhaustively lays bare the universe itself; to "comprehend,"
in the strongest sense of the word. When he wrote that
Mallarmé had undertaken in the *Coup de dés* "to raise a
printed page to the power of the midnight sky,"[55] he was
pointing, I think, to the distinctively philosophical project
that strangest of poems implies: a will to overcome the sec-
ondariness of words vis-à-vis the world—to furnish a sufficient account of what is that thereby becomes the world's
double, elevating words to the rank of things. Mallarmé's
extremest ambition, avowed in the plan to write an insurmountable Book, is the longed-for transmutation of the authority of poetry into the authority of metaphysics. Thus the
"alchemy" of his art, as he himself called it. (Why was that
second-rate author Edgar Allan Poe *le cas littéraire absolu*[56]
in Mallarmé's opinion? Because Poe had in *Eureka* sought to
overtake the universe. Indeed, it may not be too much to
understand Mallarmé's notion of a Great Work of literature,
completing the labors of poetry by fulfilling the objectives of
metaphysics, as a result of his having read Poe's cosmogoni-
cal meditation.)

   Mallarmé was a poet in revolt against literature as it had
everywhere been practiced before him. His greatest disciple,
Valéry, perseveres impressively in the quarrel with poetry by
foreswearing for fifteen crucial years his practice of it.
"Rather than seeking a further nuance or complication of
style," writes Joseph Frank, "Valéry broke with literature
altogether as the first step in discovering his own literary
path."[57] The season was early autumn, the year 1892, the
place Genoa, where he had journeyed with his parents. In
imitation—surely—of the ecstatic evening during which
Descartes had formulated his *mirabilis scientiae funda-
menta,* young Valéry stays up late of a stormy night: "I
resolved to think with rigor—to *not believe*—to consider as
null and void everything that could not be brought to total

precision."[58] The model of rationality here is mathematics, beside whose stringency poems seem an unacceptable "sacrifice of intellect." Literature fails to acquit itself at the bar of scientific seriousness. Poetry proves incompatible with the new standard of rigor. His Cartesian legacy silences Valéry, the poet, at twenty-two. He embraces mathematics as "the essential and unique object,"[59] the immaculate grammar and Orphic explanation to which everything else must be sacrificed.

An indifferent student of law at Montpellier, he there chances to meet a self-dedicated young man, Pierre Louÿs, who introduces him to another of that same stock, André Gide. Valéry avails himself of holidays to visit Paris, where he knows his future to lie. In 1894 he comes to the capital to stay, setting up in lodgings on rue Gay-Lussac. He starts in on the first of the two hundred fifty-seven notebooks he will ultimately fill. Represented by only a handful of published poems—of which, he claims, there will be no more—he presents himself to the literary great of the age: Huysmans, Heredia, Mallarmé. He confides his reflections daily to the notebook. He attends the Lamoureux concerts. Above all, he does nothing:

Nothing visible. My friends began not to understand. Even I did not know where I was headed. . . . But enormous mental activity. I studied mathematics, but in a very odd spirit, as a *model* of acts of the mind.[60]

Crossing the Alma Bridge one afternoon with Mallarmé, he remarks that he has "dreamed of a man with the greatest gifts—who would do nothing with them, being sure that he had them. . . . I said to him that it would be a fine gesture to reject the gift one is sure of having, and to seek . . . something else."[61]

At about this time Juliette Adam, editor of *La Nouvelle Revue*, invites Valéry to contribute an essay on Leonardo. The resulting work, "Introduction to the Method of Leonardo da Vinci," sounds his ground bass for a lifetime.[62] Declaring the historical Leonardo irrelevant, he posits an absolute cognitive acumen, a self miraculously superior, and calls it "Leonardo." His purpose, he insists, is pure hypothesis. About the chronologies, catalogues raisonnés, and anecdotes on which the Leonardo scholar typically depends, he writes,

My task above all is to omit them, so that a conjecture based on very general terms may in no way be confused with the visible fragments of a personality completely vanished, leaving us equally convinced both of his thinking existence and of the impossibility of ever knowing it better.[63]

Not the self that comes into history but "the potential self," as he will later call it, is Valéry's subject. Thirty-six years after writing the article for Mme. Adam, he will add in a scholium, "Man and Leonardo were the names I gave to what then impressed me as being the power of the mind."[64] The vaunted method of Leonardo turns out to be, quite simply, his mind, and his mind turns out to be mind as such— unvitiated by the particulars of selfhood, raised to the status of an insurmountable law.

The twenty-two-year-old Valéry finds in da Vinci's *Hostinato Rigore*—his obstinate rigor—a central enabling attitude worthy of the name method. It is the gift for seizing on connections unavailable to other minds that makes a man rigorous in this sense. Disorder is for Valéry a function of discontinuity. And here is the kingdom of his Maestro. Wherever the understanding is stayed by voids, Leonardo introduces the prodigies of his mind. His intelligence reconstitutes the world, forging continuities by a ceaseless power to wed the disparate forms of nature:

He passes from the headlong or seemingly retarded movement of the avalanche and landslide, from massive curves to multitudinous draperies; from smoke sprouting on roofs to distant tree-forms, to the vaporous beeches of the horizon; from fish to birds; from the sea glittering in the sun to birch leaves in their slender mirrors;

from scales and shells to the gleams that sail over gulfs; from ears and ringlets to the frozen whorls of the nautilus. From the shell he proceeds to the spiral tumescence of the waves; from the skin on the water of shallow pools to the veins that would warm it, and thence to the elemental movements of crawling, to the fluid serpent. He vivifies. He molds the water round a swimmer into clinging scarves, draperies that show the effort of the muscles in relief. As for the air, he transfixes it in the wake of soaring larks as ravelings of shadow; it is pictured in the frothy flights of bubbles which these aerial journeys and delicate breaths must disturb and leave trailing across the blue-tinted pages of space, the dense vague crystal of space.[65]

The mind of Leonardo passes without stint from disorder to order by means of its unfailing gift for *analogy*. Discontinuity is overcome by "our faculty of changing images, of making part of one co-exist with part of another, and of perceiving, voluntarily or involuntarily, the connections in their structure."[66] What, anyhow, is the mind but a progression of metaphors substituted one for the other? "In this way, what was not possible becomes so."[67]

Yet in the midst of so much brooding on the forms of nature and so much penetration into their complex instability—not to mention a production that includes plans for churches, fortresses, trivial entertainments, baubles, mechanical contraptions of every kind and, of course, paintings such as Florence had never beheld—he retains "the charm of always seeming to think of something else."[68] Valuing nothing above consciousness, Valéry posits an absolute instance of it in the man whose endeavors are sufficiently various to demand an account in more-than-human terms. "I propose to imagine a man," he writes at the outset of the "Introduction," "whose activities are so diverse that if I postulate a ruling idea behind them all, there could be none more universal."[69]

The "Note and Digression," his second Leonardo essay, offers an interesting contrast. Whereas the Leonardo of 1894 retains a transitive relation to the world, dissecting its parts, reconstituting its forms, the Leonardo of "Note and Digression," written a quarter-century later, has withdrawn from "the struggling mass of ordinary truths"[70] to the absolved ground of thought thinking itself. The man who, in the thick of so much doing and making, had always seemed to think of something else, becomes in "Note and Digression" the principle of lucidity, "the substantial awareness," the pure I or mind within the mind, the inner law sufficient to itself, no longer dependent for its identity on what it discovers or invents. Disjunct from every act, superior to any object, genius thus evades the world.

"In my outer darkness," Valéry writes, looking backward to the 1894 text, "I loved the inner law of the great Leonardo. I was not interested in his biography, nor even the productions of his mind. Of that brow loaded with laurels, I dreamed only of the *kernel*."[71] In his second Leonardo essay, Valéry imagines the da Vincian heaven of the mind in terms of an invariable standard, a principle of consciousness logically prior to any object encountered:

The characteristic of man is consciousness; and that of consciousness is a perpetual emptying, a process of detachment without cease or exception from anything presented to it, whatever that thing may be. An inexhaustible act, independent of the quality as of the quantity of things presented; an act by which the *man of intellect* must finally reduce himself, deliberately, to an indefinite refusal to be anything whatsoever.[72]

Except, that is, what he invariably remains: consciousness as such. If we encounter mind only in the trappings of personality, we may yet extrapolate mind in its nakedness. The invincible core, dependent on nothing beyond itself, detached or detachable from every object of reflection, is Valéry's "universal pronoun," a perspicuity that, like the cogito of Descartes, affirms itself by reference to itself alone. Divested of the corruptive traits of individuality, of the whole experience of the self as accidental, consciousness discloses the inner law validating an order of being beyond the merely existential. Consciousness as such—pure consciousness—has neither past nor future, inasmuch as its independence from outward circumstance bears it harmless and unmodified through time. For if it is the nature of a self qua personality to define itself in relation to others and to things made, done, or endured, it is the nature of the pure I to do nothing at all, to reside instead in an intransitive calm, unperturbed by memory or prospect, unacquainted with vicissitude.

None of which is to suggest that Valéry characterizes the pure mind as immortal. It is, as we would expect, coextensive with the body. But death comes to it not, as it comes to a personality, to confer meaning or completion. Only that which has had a history can be culminated in the moment of extinction. Pure consciousness, self-same in every human head, untroubled by time, is rendered no more meaningful or intelligible by its conclusion.

There is, avowedly then, a god in Valéry's house. From the myriad of idols, one of which must be worshipped, he selects the da Vincian *Hostinato Rigore.* "What could be more seductive," he writes,

than a god who rejects mystery; who does not base his power on the agitation of our senses, or address his power to the darkest, most tender, most sinister part of our natures; who forces our minds to agree, not to submit; whose miracle is to clarify and whose profundity is a carefully deduced perspective? Is there any surer sign of a real and legitimate power than its not being exercised under a veil?[73]

In the spirit of Descartes, Valéry has asked, What persists in the mind? "What is it that resists the fascination of the senses, the dissipation of ideas, the fading of memories, the slow variation of the organism, the incessant and multiform action of the universe?"[74] His answer is, of course, the autonomy of the cogito, an uncircumstanced lucidity amid the wool and welter of ordinary mental life, whose rigor consists in an independence from whatever appears to it. Consciousness as such scouts every object in favor of its preferred condition of self-reflexivity. The labor ordinary intelligence "devotes to an object of reflection" Valéry's *res cogitans* expends instead "on the subject that reflects."[75]

The fundamental categories here are not truth versus falsity, but rather seeming versus nothingness, as Cioran has remarked.[76] Valéry saves himself from the full Nietzschean encounter with nihilism by worshipping a graven image or semblance that he knows to be nothing more. Its falsity does not dissuade him. Mind as such is the beloved image in the pool—an untruth, an idol. Bending to it, like Narcissus, he adores only what is not, only "the strange omnipotence of the nil."[77] Likewise, Valéry's putative heroes of possibility, his exemplary geniuses—Teste, Leonardo, Descartes—stand more profoundly for all we *cannot* do or be. Each is an apparition masking a void. Pure consciousness, indeed: *"Pure, meaning the sign of nothing."*[78] Valéry rebukes humanness with the semblance thus conjured. "Only when we are thinking of nothing," he writes in the notebooks, "do we really think of ourselves."[79]

Only the void creates. "The proper, unique and constant object of thought," he says, *"is that which does not exist."*[80] Now, to insist on semblance as our fit nourishment is to insist on the food of the gods. This Valéry does every time. But having furnished forth the heavenly table, he bids us drink deep with him from the bitter mixed cup of our worldliness.

The projects of metaphysics have used up their credit, says Valéry. Yet we may "save the noumena"; we may admire intrinsic beauties of the metaphysical systems apart from any truth value. What motivated metaphysics in the first place? "The passion for conceiving everything that exists,"[81] as Valéry puts it in "Leonardo and the Philosophers" (1929), his third and final essay on da Vinci. "We might picture philosophy," he writes,

as the attitude of concentration and restraint owing to which some-one, at moments, thinks his life or lives his thinking in a sort of equivalence, or in a reversible state, between being and *knowing*— while he tries to suspend all conventional expression and waits eagerly for a combination much more precious than the others to take shape and reveal itself, a combination of the reality he feels impelled to offer with the reality he is able to receive.[82]

Now, a reversible state between being and knowing would be what we mean by truth. But alert as he was to developments in the physical sciences, Valéry understood that in their do-mains, no less than in philosophy, the naïve assumption of truth as correspondence or equivalence between what is and what is thought cannot withstand inspection:

We are witnessing an extraordinary phenomenon: the very develop-ment of the sciences is tending to weaken the concept of Knowl-edge. I mean that a seemingly impregnable area of science, one that it shared with philosophy (in other words, with faith in the intelligible and belief in the inherent value of mental acquisitions) is gradually yielding ground to a new fashion of conceiving or evalu-ating the function of cognition. No longer can the effort of the intellect be regarded as converging toward an intellectual limit, toward the *True*.[83]

Stupendous successes in the sciences, no less than the de-mise of metaphysics, point to the dissolution of an indemni-fied standard. Physical laws come to be reinterpreted as rules that are binding only at the given level of experiment or observation. *Success* replaces truth as the standard:

Science consists, I would say, of the total sum of formulas and processes that are invariably successful, and it is coming progres-sively closer to being a table of correspondences between human actions and phenomena, an always longer and more definite table of such correspondences, recorded in the most precise and economical systems of notation. Infallibility in prediction is, in simple fact, the only characteristic that modern man regards as having more than a conventional value. He is tempted to say, "All the rest is literature."[84]

What the Greeks called *theōria*, the pure act of metaphysical contemplation, loses all claim on meaning, inasmuch as it implies "a contemplator different in essence from ourselves," a knower who is not also the shaper of whatever he knows. Which, then, of our propositions are meaningful? Which pass muster as clear and distinct? Only those that experiment goes on corroborating. The rest is literature—sacrifice of intellect:

Knowledge of this sort is never separated from action or from instruments of execution or control, without which, moreover, *it has no meaning*—whereas if it is based on them, if it refers back to them at every moment, it enables us to deny meaning to knowledge of any other sort.[85]

He writes "Leonardo and the Philosophers" in order to put forward da Vinci as first to have lived and worked in accordance with this criterion of meaningfulness. Leonardo, hero of the anti-metaphysical stance—in this way, Valéry ascribes to his Maestro the disabused modern mind he in fact prides himself on.

Where does this positivism—for we must call it that—stem from? Nietzsche, not Comte. Valéryan, like Nietzschean, truth is comprised of all those falsehoods we cannot expose as such, cannot not believe in. Valéryan truth is any bridge that spans the void and bears our weight.

He made a point throughout his career of reviling Pascal, greatest of all French thinkers. Why? Because Pascal, rather than flinging his bridge across the void, looked down and saw terror there. The true pagan, Valéry once said, is distinguished by his conviction that no one thing is worth the whole of his being. He despised—or maybe feared—Pascal precisely for having concluded from the experience of nothingness that one thing only is needful. "This infinite abyss can be filled only with an infinite object," as the *Pensées* implacably argues.

For all that he would have denied it, Valéry's sleepless night at Genoa, overtly imitative of Descartes' night of reason, may be more profoundly linked to a different event, Pascal's plenitudinous night of faith:

The year of grace 1654. Monday, 23 November. . . . From about half past ten in the evening until half past midnight. Fire. . . . Certainty, certainty, heartfelt joy, peace. . . . The world forgotten, and everything except God. . . . Greatness of the human soul. . . . Joy, joy, joy, tears of joy. . . . And this is life eternal.

The author of these famous words of mystical affirmation, who was one of the five or six best mathematical and scientific minds of the seventeenth century, derided Pico della Mirandola for having entitled a work *On All That Can Be Known*. Assuredly not because he doubted the efficacy of knowledge. But what he did doubt—and more than doubt— was its power to save us. As comprehensively learned as anyone in Europe, Pascal laughed at attempts to make a *gnosis* of mere learning, whether scientific or humane. There is no heaven of the intellect, he argued; there is only our need of grace. What can be known amounts to no more than "an imperceptible dot in nature's ample bosom." If reason were reasonable, it would give up the vanity of attempting to know all the rest. "Reason's last step," Pascal wrote, "is the recognition that there is an infinite number of things beyond it. It is merely feeble if it does not go so far as to realize that." This is why atheism—one of reason's notable works— signifies strength of mind only up to a point, beyond which it may perhaps signify blindness and folly. For reason can furnish only propositions. Behind these, to first principles, reason cannot go.

Propositions are proved; principles are felt. Reason tries in vain to confute those first principles to which the heart inclines. For example, that we have lost our true nature. This condition of loss—called original sin—is irrefutable to those who feel it. Much as grace, its opposite and antidote, is irrefutable. In other words, the matter of our "whence," no less than of our "whither," lies beyond the competence of intellect. Such is the scandal of the cogito or reason. Without God's revelation in the first book of Holy Writ, we should be ciphers to ourselves, powerless to account for the breathtaking versatility of evil in us, unable even to recognize that we are fallen, not as we ought to be.

We've lost our true nature and there lies frightfulness, for anything can now become our nature. This argument of Pascal's is based not on reason but rather on the heart's intuition. We've lost our true nature, and mind as such is powerless to restore it. So it is not within ourselves that we find what is needful, even if the various humanisms would have it so. Where they put the *Wissensdrang* that sets a man free, gains him his new life, Pascal puts only our insurmountable need of grace. When he has occasion to speak, as he surely does, of the *grandeur* of man, what he affirms is but a contingent greatness, held in equipoise with misery. Not, to be sure, the *misère* of dumb animals, but rather of a great lord, a dispossessed king. Is one not reminded of Paul Valéry, who similarly declares man to be both great and abject? However, what Pascal means is that man is wretched because of what he is, great because of what, through God, he may become, whereas Valéry means that man is wretched because of what he is, great because of what he *imagines* himself to be. Man may evade the sense of nullity by positing apparitions or fictive giants of himself—but must come home again and again to his poverty: "Sometimes I think, and sometimes I am." What Valéry sponsors is in effect a false or imaginary sublime, freely acknowledged as such.

To which Pascal replies, "imagination cannot make fools wise, but it can make them happy." It has been said that in a dark time Paul Valéry stands for light, "a man who, in an age that worships the chaotic idols of blood, earth, and passion, preferred always the lucid pleasures of thought and the secret adventures of order."[86] This assessment by Jorge Luis Borges is just and handsome. But is there not a shadow side to Valéry's lucid pleasures? Never was an author less confessional; to lay the heart bare was not his way, not with such secrets as he had to keep, darkest of which may be that he was the froward descendant of Blaise Pascal—from whom *doubleness*, Valéry's major trope for the human, derives. "Is it not clearer than day," the author of the *Pensées* had asked, "that we feel within ourselves the indelible marks of excellence, and is it not equally true that we constantly experience the effects of our deplorable condition?" *Misère et grandeur*. What became an acknowledged fiction, a painted thing for Valéry, had been a disclaimed forebear's certitude one jubilant, fervent night. The certitude, the fiction: *l'homme passe l'homme*—man transcends man.

Chapter 3

∙ ∙ ∙

In Faust's Den:
The Lament of Freud

Auch die Kultur, die alle Welt beleckt,
Hat auf den Teufel sich erstreckt.

—Goethe

Storm troopers paid a courtesy call to Berggasse 19 in mid-March of 1938, and a week later came the Gestapo. Not a surprise to the old Galitsianer who lived there. In a letter to Arnold Zweig four years earlier, Freud had likened his life in Vienna to "waiting in a hotel room for the second shoe to be flung against the wall." On March 11, 1938, Hitler entered Austria. The second shoe had been flung.

Freud read the Anschluss, as he'd read previous outbreaks of history, by the light of his science. "You see the fact of Man as it is,"[1] Zweig had written to him in the previous summer, neatly summing up the ambition of psychoanalysis from its inception. As a science of the fact of man, Freud's theory and practice pride themselves on the abjuring of illusion. "I cannot be an optimist," he wrote to Lou Andreas Salomé during the First World War, "and I believe I differ from the pessimists only in so far as wicked, stupid, senseless things don't upset me because I have accepted them from the beginning as part of what the world is composed of."[2]

Between 1914 and 1945 seventy million people would be done to death in two world wars. Freud was witness to the European Walpurgis Night, and while he did not live to learn of its culmination in the camps where four of his own sisters would perish, he may have understood better than anybody else has the buried dynamism of our twentieth-century politics of evil, for his metapsychology grasps the *internal* nexus between barbarity and culture, between the psychic solicitations to sink and to rise.

While he would, I think, have agreed with Schopenhauer that the geniuses a civilization can produce are but the lucid intervals in an otherwise bitter tale,[3] he would doubtless have added the insistence—distinctively psychoanalytic—that the lucid interval and the bitter tale are interdependent, that the radiance and the darkness implicate each other; and that the genius is, accordingly, but a heightened instance of the fracture of man. Like us, only more so. This self-divided, self-qualifying character of genius is the self-divided, self-qualifying character of culture itself. Freud's final argument about man binds together Eros and Thanatos into a monumental myth of self-division. "Does not every science come in the end to a kind of mythology?"[4] he asked Einstein in an open letter of 1932. Freud's is a myth the century that began in August of 1914 has reason to recognize as its own. But there are potent resistances coming between us and the metapsychological theory of an instinct unto death. For within its solemn terms, the linkage between our drive to love, on the one hand, and to destroy, on the other, turns out to be more intimate than perhaps any of us can bear to believe.

He could not help looking back with nostalgia to the old century, of course. What he tended to see in our own was an unredemptive end of days. "I do not doubt," he wrote to Frau Lou in 1916,

that mankind will surmount even this war, but I know for certain that I and my contemporaries will never again see a joyous world. It is all too hideous. And the saddest thing about it is that it has come out just as from our analytic expectations we should have imagined man and his behaviour. . . . My secret conclusion was: since we can only regard the highest civilization of the present as disfigured by a gigantic hypocrisy it follows that we are organically unfitted for it. We have to abdicate, and the Great Unknown, He or It, lurking behind Fate, will sometime repeat such an experiment with another race.[5]

Freud's "secret conclusion" was that European man, like the neurotic individuals of the consultation room, had lived beyond his psychic means. European man's civilization was a splendid pretense belying the dark core. When Freud writes of Europe's "hypocrisy," he means Europe's *neurosis.* What is that? Clinically speaking, an illness that sets a soul at enmity with its own instinctual needs, repressing the drives and suffering them to be known only in a disfigured, symptomatic way. Freud saw in the Great War a huge and ghastly neurotic symptom, a return of the repressed. What the blood of Verdun and the Somme betokened for him was a collapse of the mendacious front. "Life has, in truth, become interesting again," he'd written in 1915. "It has regained its full significance."[6] Indeed, European life had gotten back to basics, shed its façade. The proud old claims of *Kultur* lay disaffirmed. A vast instinctual debt had come due, and the reckoning would be in human lives.

It is a view of what the war meant that was familiar in German-speaking culture. Decisively influenced by Freud, Thomas Mann concluded *The Magic Mountain* (1924) with a plangency that seems all but addressed to the founder of psychoanalysis: "Out of this universal feast of death, out of this extremity of fever, kindling the rainwashed evening sky to a fiery glow, may it be that Love one day shall mount?" Freud had already answered Mann's question in *Beyond the Pleasure Principle* (1920); he would answer it again in *Civilization and Its Discontents* (1930). The answer, both times, was—No. Preemption of the utopian yearning is Freud's intellectual signature. "There are few things," as Richard Wollheim writes, "that so effectively divide him from our own more enthusiastic age than his refusal to believe that it is in any way the mark of a good or generous mind to give way to hope."[7]

But the quick of Freud's understanding lies deeper than any antiutopianism, however resolute. He belongs to that tough-minded Sophoclean company for whom the wisdom of Silenus, spoken to King Midas, is final. Story goes that the king, knowing Silenus to possess the secret of what is happiness, lured the satyr to the royal garden, got him drunk, and coerced the great secret from him. What he learned is that it is best never to have been born, second best to die as quickly as possible. Seeking to crown his good fortune with wisdom, the king is instead mocked in the delusive hope that he could ever be happy. What about a view of life that seems thus to strike at the will to live? We don't know what Midas did with his fell knowledge, but he has descendants more forthcoming.

"I can't go on," Beckett writes in a famous passage. "I'll go on."

Kafka allows as there is infinite hope in the universe, but none of it for us.

The veil of *maya* lifted from his eyes, Schopenhauer sees only inanity and madness in our will to live—yet each day, prior to a bountiful lunch, plays Rossini on the flute.

"Although I continuously understand," writes Leopardi, "in fact I intensely feel, the futility of everything human, I am still grieved and disturbed by how much there is to do."

The noble exponents of pessimism are never content just to register a sense of the futility of life, though the will to live is genuinely at risk in their writings. The puzzle is always this: reared on despair, their stance is also the indemnification against despair. Cioran writes on behalf of them all, "We can endure any truth, however destructive, provided it replaces everything, provided it affords as much vitality as the hope for which it substitutes."[8] Despair as resolution.

The preponderance of evil over good as a spur to life. Pessimism as vitality. To live knowing what Silenus knows involves us in a strange exoneration from whose height suicide looks merely puerile, a mistake. Giacomo Leopardi or Samuel Beckett a suicide? Preposterous. "It's not worth the bother of killing yourself," Cioran explains, "since you always kill yourself *too late.*"[9] Once you're born, the mischief has been made.

Is this not the lesson Oedipus carries with him from Thebes? In the triumphal *tyrannos,* solver of the riddle of the Sphinx, Freud found the pattern of his own intellectual powers. In defeated, outcast Oedipus, solver of the riddle of himself, he found something else, a moral postulate on which to base his theoretical claims. Freud states this postulate simply, much in fact as a Sophoclean chorus might: "To endure life remains, when all is said, the first duty."[10] He loves in Oedipus the inexorable demand for self-discovery—but still moreso, the steadfastness to life. In the solitude of his self-analysis Freud, as doctor and patient in one, established a new pattern of the old Oedipal tenacity. By contrast to Jocasta, who prefers untruth and perishes, Oedipus abjures illusion and lives. He is blind and vagrant, true. But pain is not the end of the tale, as Freud well understood. For the knowledge Oedipus has endured at Thebes, a blessing awaits him in the sacred grove at Colonus, home of the Furies turned Kindly Ones. Freud does acknowledge a little refuge from history, a sacred grove where history is mastered. It consists of two people and—potentially—a blessing: the psychoanalytic situation.

The psychoanalytic situation implies a superior and a subordinate. Between analyst and analysand there exists an inequality it is the function of analysis to remedy. Freud's mature technique is an educative strategy whereby the patient's resistances to unconscious material—the loves and hates and reprehended wishes of early childhood—are in due course wrested from him. "The analyst," writes Jürgen Habermas,

> instructs the patient in reading his own texts, which he himself has mutilated and distorted, and in translating symbols from a mode of expression deformed as a private language into the mode of expression as public communication.

The analyst, that is, teaches the analysand a way of unriddling himself:

> At the end of analysis it should be possible to present narratively those events of the forgotten years of life that neither the patient nor the analyst knew at the beginning of the analysis. . . . Only the patient's recollection decides the accuracy of the construction. If it applies, it must also "restore" to the patient a portion of lost life history: that is, it must be able to elicit a self-reflection.[11]

Analysis delivers up to the prudential order of the ego what otherwise could not make its way into consciousness: the prehistoric emotions and the internalized system of inhibitions by which these are held in check.

The conceptual keystone here is repression—*Verdrängung*—the censorial mechanism acting to disown dangerous impulses and to consign them to the netherside of consciousness. Patients enter analysis because they are suffering. They are suffering because of unconscious—that is, repressed—conflicts between instinct and inhibition. These conflicts are called *neuroses*, the spawn of our early and catastrophic adventures in love.

In "Analysis Terminable and Interminable" (1937), a magisterial statement of therapeutic purpose, Freud likens repression to the textual deletions made by certain ancient and medieval scribes:

> The offensive passages were heavily scored through so that they were illegible . . . could not be transcribed and the next copyist of the book produced a text to which no exception could be taken but which had gaps in certain places. . . . Repression is to the other

methods of defence what the omission of words or passages is to the corruption of a text, and in the various forms of this falsification we can discover parallels to the manifold ways in which the ego can be modified.[12]

These modifications—usually called defense mechanisms or resistances—by which the ego protects itself from unwelcome truths, become important texts for the doctor and his patient. The latter is instructed by the fundamental rule of their compact to say whatever comes into his head; and yet he cannot; unconscious resistances within the ego itself keep him from doing so. Freud noted from the outset this typical inability of his patients to free associate, but only much later did he come to theorize about it. Psychoanalysis began as a symptom-treating therapy. But as its focus gradually shifted from the repressed contents of the mind to the ego mechanisms that *keep* reprehended ideas and affects out of consciousness, Freudian practice modified itself into a character-altering therapy requiring not months but years of intensive sessions. The essential turn was away from the premise of depth psychology—that the patient free associating his way back to secreted impulses could, by bringing these to consciousness, deprive the pathogenic elements of their force, what became Freud's new focus was the repressing forces themselves that consistently kept patients from obeying the fundamental rule.

He did not abandon depth psychology, of course. But he came to believe that an analysis of the repressing forces was at least as important as analysis of the repressed itself. So it was that in the last phase of his work he tended to understand treatment as a tacking between depth and ego psychologies. Freud writes in the late essay already quoted,

Our theoretical work swings to and fro during the treatment like a pendulum, analysing now a fragment of the id and now a fragment of the ego. In the one case our aim is to bring a part of the id into consciousness and in the other to correct something in the ego. The crux of the matter is that the mechanisms of defence against former dangers recur in analysis in the shape of *resistances to cure*.[13]

What recur, also, in every psychoanalytic situation, are new editions of the old child-parent relationships. The patient unwittingly repeats, "acts out" vis-à-vis his doctor in the here and now, a forgotten but ever operative drama of the remote past. This repetition Freud calls the *transference*, and far from seeing it merely as a feature of the consultation room, he came to regard all strong personal relationships as transferential, our loves as well as our hatreds shadowed by the emotional agendas of childhood.

The therapeutic significance of the transference cannot be overstated. Freud in fact believed that a treatment only deserves the name psychoanalysis if, as he puts it in "Beginning the Treatment" (1913), "the intensity of the transference has been utilized for the overcoming of resistances."[14] This can happen only when the repetitive pattern of acting out is broken and replaced by *remembering*, for the resistances to cure are fundamentally resistances to memory. Transference is repetition. And it is only through the exacting process of what Freud calls "working through" that the analysand can be led of his own will to recognize, in his comportment toward his analyst, the loves and hatreds of early life.

It is, then, from what the patient's emotions demand in the present from his doctor, along with his unwitting stratagems for disobeying the fundamental rule of free association, that both doctor and patient may draw the most telling conclusions about what happened in the latter's early years. A new epistemological category is thus born: *psychoanalytic knowledge*, whose truth is, as Janet Malcolm has written, that "of what the present betrays about the past."[15] Rather than the historicist ideal of reconstruction—Ranke's *wie es eigentlich gewesen ist*—this new notion of truth serves doctor and patient as a directing standard: not the past as it really happened, but the past insofar as it survives to make mischief in the present. "It may indeed be questioned," Freud writes in "Screen Memories" (1899),

> whether we have any memories at all *from* our childhood: memories *relating to* our childhood may be all that we possess. Our childhood memories show us our earliest years not as they were but as they appeared at the later periods when the memories were revived. In these periods of revival, the childhood memories did not, as people are accustomed to say, *emerge;* they were *formed* at that time. And a number of motives, which had no concern with historical accuracy, had their part in thus forming them as well as in the selection of the memories themselves.[16]

Superficial resemblances notwithstanding, psychoanalytic science is no ally of the historical sciences. It does not care about the past for its own sake. "The patient in analysis," writes French analyst O. Mannoni, "does not bend over his past like an old man writing his memoirs. He is less occupied with restoring his past than with going beyond it, which is the only real way of preserving it."[17] Psychoanalysis goes athwart the past in order to bring about a change in the present: namely, to widen the scope and discretionary powers of the ego—*das Ich*—on all its fronts, tempering involuntary drives with deliberate responses, unconscious prohibitions with self-knowing prudence. "A psychoanalysis," Freud writes, "is not an impartial scientific investigation, but a therapeutic measure. Its essence is not to prove anything, but . . . to alter something."[18]

If less pessimistic about the consultation room than about the world, he was nonetheless quick to insist that therapeutic results are far from easy or guaranteed. The new and stronger synthesis of the ego which analysis seeks to instate is a poise of spirit never spontaneously attained to; rather, it is the always contingent end result of a prolonged, arduous, and rule-governed labor of inquiry. Where id was, analyst and patient together install the reign of self-knowledge, of deliberation—of ego. And on the strength of this gain in self-knowledge, analytic practice bases its claim to have healed.

It is now more than thirty years since Norman O. Brown suggested, in his influential book *Life against Death*, that "psychoanalytic consciousness, as a higher stage in the consciousness of mankind, may be . . . the fulfillment of the historical consciousness, that ever widening and deepening search for origins that has obsessed Western thought since the Renaissance."[19]

What has impelled us backward to our sources? Brown's answer is that our historicism represents a slow return of the repressed, our secret progressively more exposed, nearer in its manifestation "to the original impulse and to the original forbidden act itself."[20] Our search for origins is for Brown a symptom of our modernity. What, then, is the repressed content of historicism, our backward impetus? A less and less well-buried urge, Brown says, to be quit of the past, to lay down the burden of history. For history is the story of repression: history *is* neurosis—the neurosis of the species—and man, the historical animal, is by that token the animal who is sick.

Historical processes are engendered and sustained by a human wish to be other, to make of the given place another place and of the given self another self. And here, according to Brown, is the unconscious of history, the intent it keeps hidden from its makers. Apocalyptic visionary that he is, Brown forecasts a resolution of historical consciousness— the hold of what comes earlier over what comes later—into "psychoanalytical consciousness," the escape into an unmediated present. Historical consciousness he sees as a symptom of the disease called man at a late stage. As with the burden every patient brings to analysis so, according to Brown, with the burden we bring to modernity: the way out is through. Historical consciousness must be aggravated, completed so that it may in the end defeat itself, break apart to yield up, beyond the last weariness of history, a renovated human nature. "If historical consciousness is finally transformed into psychoanalytical consciousness," Brown writes,

the grip of the dead hand of the past on life in the present would be loosened, and man would be ready to live instead of making history, to enjoy instead of paying back old scores and debts, and to enter that state of Being which was the goal of his becoming.[21]

Life against Death (like the whole of Brown's subsequent career) is the seeking of a way out of repression as the precondition of culture. Fixing his sights on a future in which civilization will no longer levy its instinctual toll (and man no longer be "the sick animal," as Nietzsche called him) Brown declares the prospect of a life based on the free play of the instincts. Where Philip Rieff has seen the era of "psychological man," Brown has seen the portal to an apocalypse in whose aftertime the labor of spirit will no longer involve us in fracture and self-division, no longer exact the displacement from below to above.

That is to say, no longer require *sublimation*, the psychic process by which instinctual energy is turned from sexual to cultural aims. Freud found in it the intrapsychic representative of art, science, spirit—of all that is higher. Intelligence was, as he saw it, the cumulative result not of any purported "instinct toward perfection" in the species, but rather of the desexualizing trend of the mind that makes us culture-producing animals in the first place. The displacement from the solipsistic to the shared, from flesh to spirit, creates the conditions of culture out of a negation, a repression of the original satisfactions that we are compelled to relinquish in early childhood. In their stead, the ego proposes to itself the substitute satisfactions of the spirit: sublimations.

Culture is, in Freud's view, an elaborate consolation—and a costly one. For if repressions are the condition of sublimation, then we may expect them to take their gradual revenge on culture itself. Freud writes in *The Ego and the Id* (1923),

> By . . . getting hold of the libido from the object-cathexes and desex-
> ualizing or sublimating the libido of the id, the ego is working in
> opposition to the purposes of Eros and placing itself at the service of
> the opposing instinctual impulses.[22]

When turned inward, these impulses are called the death
drive by Freud in *Beyond the Pleasure Principle*; when
turned outward, they are called aggression. A dualist
throughout his career, Freud in his last phase replaces the
opposition of self-protective or ego instincts to sexual instincts with a new opposition of Eros to death. Freud's final
theory of the drives assimilates the self-preservative to the
erotic; what the new dualism announced in 1920 posits over
against the drive to love, to make more of life, is an antithetical drive to cancel, to dissolve, to obliterate, and thus to
recover what Schopenhauer called "the lost paradise of non-
existence."[23]

These two primordial instincts are always found in combination, Freud argues. When in the twenties and thirties he
writes *Trieb*, Freud means Eros as alloyed by death. What
disturbs him in *The Ego and the Id* is the particular way they
combine in sublimation, after which "the erotic component
no longer has the power to bind the whole of the destructiveness that was combined with it, and this is released in the
form of an inclination to aggression and destruction."[24]

Or, alternatively, in the form of a will to master. Freud
had already in 1915 identified an impulse of cruelty at the
bottom of every instinct for control.[25] Five years later he
would see in that impulse the death instinct turned outward.
When Freud speaks of the drive for mastery, he of course has
his eye on its most favorable versions, science and art. But
they, too, no less than masterings of the more basic kind,
would seem in Freud's account to bear an intrinsic relation
to aggressiveness or destruction. Already in 1915, he has
begun to discern *within* culture a gainsaying countertrend.

His final theory of the instincts, by putting death in opposition to Eros, thereby puts it in opposition to the claims

of culture. For these claims, Freud argues throughout the twenties, are the selfsame objectives of Eros in its struggle with death. Culture, like love, comes to stand for the perpetual "renewal of life,"[26] inasmuch as the aim of culture, as of Eros, is the unification of life into ever larger units. Intellect, science, and art unite, even as the more fundamental forms of civilization (agriculture, technology, law). But sublimation, the psychic process whereby energies are made available to the purposes of culture, brings unexpectedly in its train the old enemy principle of strife and disunion. In the process of displacement from a sexual to a nonsexual aim, aggressiveness is released from its subordination to libidinal trends. Thus, in Freud's final reckoning, culture casts the shadow of its opposite—as surely as love casts the *hadow of hate.

Any attempt, like Norman O. Brown's, to read the human story as romance must answer Freud's determination to read it as irreconcilable conflict, as tragedy. For Freud's dialectic of Eros and death brooks no resolution. He was the founding teacher of a discipline of healing; and yet it may be as a rabbi of the irremediable, like Kafka, that he shall figure largest. It may be as a man *without* answers that we shall need Freud most.

America bemused and embarrassed him, perhaps because he could not take seriously a culture founding itself on the right of individuals to be happy. Indeed, the happiness of the individual is, according to his metapsychology, what civilization always subordinates to its grander scheme. "America," he explained to Ernest Jones, "is a mistake."[27]

Crossing the Atlantic for the first and last time in the autumn of 1909 to deliver a series of introductory lectures at Clark University, Freud worried aloud on board the *George Washington*, the ocean liner bringing him here, that in America psychoanalysis would be perverted into a panacea, its antithetical content forgotten. Years later when Samuel

Goldwyn, that addict of happy endings, came to Vienna to try luring Freud to Hollywood as a scriptwriter and on-the-set advisor, the father of psychoanalysis must have had his worst suspicions about us confirmed. "There are some people," Goldwyn complained afterward, "you can't tell them a goddam thing. Like him. Freud."[28]

The man you couldn't tell a goddam thing certainly didn't see himself as introducing a recipe for happiness to the United States. "We are bringing them the plague,"[29] he said. But Freud did concede in his last Clark lecture, perhaps partly out of deference to the host country, that "the satisfaction of the individual's happiness cannot be erased from among the aims of our civilization." He went on to tell a story about the little German town of Schilda, whose citizens decided to break their workhorse of his bad habit of consuming so many oats. They gradually reduced the beast's rations to the point where he was eating only one stalk a day. But on the morning he was deprived of even this, the workhorse spitefully lay down and died. Moral: a body needs its oats. "The plasticity of the components of sexuality," Freud said to his American audience,

shown by their capacity for sublimation, may indeed offer a great temptation to strive for still greater cultural achievements by still greater sublimation. But, just as we do not count on our machines converting more than a certain fraction of the heat consumed into useful mechanical work, we ought not to seek to alienate the whole amount of the energy of the sexual instinct from its proper ends. We cannot succeed in doing so; and if the restriction on sexuality were to be carried too far it would inevitably bring with it all the evils of soil exhaustion.[30]

He seems to have returned to Europe preoccupied by this issue of desexualization; as soon as the *Five Lectures* was readied for print he turned himself in earnest to it. The result, in May of 1910, was *Leonardo da Vinci and a Memory of His Childhood*, Freud's most sustained attempt to give content to the idea of sublimation.

"How nicely," says Nietzsche's Zarathustra, "the bitch, sensuality, knows how to beg for a piece of spirit when denied a piece of meat."[31] Sublimation is this precisely: the substitution of spirit for meat. And Freud proposes his Leonardo to stand for the heroism of that displacement upward. But his da Vinci must also be understood as standing for the tragic contradictions embedded in culture as psychoanalysis will ultimately conceive it. For Freud, Leonardo is the limit case of sublimation and all its sorrows. Freud's Leonardo is an unhappy man, and for Freud it is this unhappiness that sets the seal of genius on him, makes of da Vinci *the* culture hero.

The *Leonardo* is a work as tense with ambivalence as any he wrote. In the immensity of da Vinci's spirit—given over first to art, then to scientific research in the service of his painting, still later to research at the expense of his art, and finally to painting once again—Freud perceives the steady elaboration of a self-undermining impulse. His wish to find in Leonardo the replete embodiment of cultural values, of sublimated energy, comes up against the record of Leonardo's procrastination and inability to make decisions, his frequent refusal to finish works, his disastrous choice of a medium for the *Last Supper*, and so on. In the end Freud is obliged to see in his invented hero a being irremediably self-divided. Having stated in the first chapter that this will be a case study in "the perfection of the great," Freud is moved by the last to stamp his Leonardo with "the tragic mark of failure." The book belies its own fervent wish that the scientific exercise of the will to truth might constitute a principle of freedom and health, an escape from historically rooted instinctual conflicts into a life unfraught with the new editions of old contests between instinct and inhibition. Instead, Freud's Leonardo carries the whole sickening burden of his past into the fortress of the intellect with him.

Ten years after the *Leonardo*, Freud writes in *Beyond the Pleasure Principle,*

It may be difficult . . . for many of us to abandon the belief that there is an instinct towards perfection at work in human beings, which has brought them to their present high level of intellectual achievement and ethical sublimation and which may be expected to watch over their development into supermen.[32]

But this was a naïvely self-flattering belief Freud felt we *must* abandon. He would have nothing to do with any "supposititious instinct towards perfection" in human nature. Twenty years after the *Leonardo* he writes, "We have been careful not to fall in with the prejudice that civilization is synonymous with perfecting, that it is the road to perfection preordained for men."[33] And yet Freud shared Nietzsche's faith in "men who are destinies, who by bearing themselves bear destinies"—incommensurable men, "the whole species of *heroic* bearers of burdens."[34]

Freud's oblique pronouncements on genius may best be understood, I think, as fragments of an autobiography. Indeed, his *self-analysis*—the constitutive event in the history of his science—becomes for him the very pattern of genius. Without benefit of preexisting concepts or techniques, Freud undertook in 1897 to fathom his own hiddenmost self. Afterward, he declared this solitary labor of self-interpretation to be unique and unrepeatable. As Philip Rieff has written, "Freud reserved to himself, as he who first found the way, the skill to dismantle his own dreams accurately without another's aid. Nobody psychoanalyzed the first psychoanalyst."[35]

With this unaccountable, unrepeatable feat, Freud believed himself to have taken his place in that republic of geniuses of which Schopenhauer spoke. As he puts it in "On the History of the Psychoanalytic Movement" (1914), "I was one of those who have disturbed the sleep of the world."[36] Freud understood the cultural achievement, the *Kulturarbeit*, of his self-analysis as a testament of incommensurability. Here we gain a crucial insight into what genius meant to him, for it is always in his view the inexplicably great culture work that validates claims to the highest title. His youthful wish for genius, so evident in the early letters to friends and to his fiancée, is only realized in the exercise of a new form of self-interrogation, a *Wissensdrang* entirely of his own devising. That process of introspection results in a literary masterpiece, *The Interpretation of Dreams* (1899–1900) and represents Freud's emergence, at the age of forty-four, into mastery.

But how is his sense of his own genius related to his sense of Leonardo's? His "analysis" of da Vinci amounts, by his own admission, to a kind of "psychoanalytic novel"—an apologue about *Kulturarbeit* and its woes. Leonardo is Freud's symbol at midcareer for what, twenty years later, he will call the inevitable discontent or unease *(das Unbehagen)* of the culture-producing animal.

The sacrifices culture imposes have their epitome, for Freud, in the sacrifices of genius, which is for him, as it was for Schopenhauer, the ultimate justification of culture. But genius is for Freud, as it was not for Schopenhauer, an outsize mirror in which we may see all the confrontations of psychic life giantly recapitulated. Read from the vantage point *Civilization and Its Discontents* provides, Freud's Leonardo begins to look like a first version of the war between primal Yes and primal No, beween Eros and death. In the text of 1930, Freud's earlier ambivalence about sublimation has turned into a profound pessimism. What had once been seen as a "way out, a way in which the claims of the ego can be met without involving repression,"[37] has become by the last decade of Freud's career a psychical process contaminated from the outset by the specter of internalized aggression. Sublimation implies the renouncing of instinct. Instinct, by the latter part of Freud's career, always means Eros as alloyed by death. But after energy is displaced, after libido is desexualized, the element of aggression that was compact with it evades, at least in part, the hegemony of Eros and pursues a course of its own as self-destructiveness.

To grasp this stern line of thought, one must first appreciate the innovation in Freud's metapsychology represented by the 1914 paper "On Narcissism: An Introduction." From this point onward, he understands libido essentially as narcissistic overflow. As he explains in 1923, "The ego is to be regarded as the great reservoir of libido from which libido is sent out *to* objects and which is always ready to absorb libido flowing back *from* objects."[38] This reconception of libido as fundamentally narcissistic enables the refinement in the concept of sublimation that we find in *The Ego and the Id*. Freud there argues that before libidinal energy can be desexualized and thereby transmuted into cultural energy, it must first go through an intermediate phase in which object-libido is returned to the reservoir of the ego. But it is just here that the ego enters into complicity with the silent drive to destruction. For the ego cannot desexualize the libido of the id without consigning to repression the destructiveness that was combined with it. And that destructiveness thenceforth has a new, howbeit unconscious, life of its own. Freud argues in *The Ego and the Id* what he had refused to concede outright in the *Leonardo* but later assumes in *Civilization and Its Discontents:* that the sublimations never are "perfect," that they always involve a return of the repressed.

In the 1910 book Freud had gingerly asserted that in scientific inquiry, highest of the sublimations, "the libido evades the fate of repression by being sublimated from the very beginning into curiosity and by becoming attached to the powerful instinct for research as a reinforcement."[39] But by 1930 he has come round to Ferenczi's point if view: that sublimations satisfy the instincts only to the same degree maps satisfy the wish to travel. As I see it, the poignance of the *Leonardo* is its theoretical instability. I would argue that the book's overt (and very Schopenhauerian) deprecation of happiness in favor of heroism is countervailed by a submerged argument interpreting those fantastical smiles of the

Mona Lisa, the Virgin, the Baptist as so many rebukes to the all-too-human in us settling for a trade-off of flesh for spirit. Against the vertical axis along which instinct is transcended, Freud shadows forth in his *Leonardo* a horizontal axis along which fantasy proliferates despite sublimation. Because Eros implies a mobility, a transitiveness of the self, it must be the effort of civilization, as Leo Bersani has put it, "to plot the immobilization of desire."[40] Thus Freud "plots" his Leonardo; but the horizontal productivity of Eros goes on of its own accord. For if fantasy has its origins, as Freud argues, in an irrecoverable experience of bliss at the mother's breast, then all later gratifications must be incomplete and include an ulterior supplement that does not find discharge. Sex is bound, then, to fail of its aim, inasmuch as it remains always a circle of partial satisfactions.

As I've indicated, after 1920 Freud introduces into this circle, into every instance of desiring, a principle beyond that of pleasure. The maintenance of tensions at a level of constancy gets bound up, in the new metapsychology, with a more primordial tendency, one shared by all animate matter: to reduce tensions to zero, to return to the pre-organic state. Hence desire gets riddled throughout, in Freud's second or "structural" topography of the mind, with the ultimate fantasy proffering an absolute end to all desire: nirvana. Santayana writes in his essay on *Beyond the Pleasure Principle*:

> We must not confuse the itch which our unsatisfied instincts continue to cause with the pleasure of satisfying and dismissing each of them in turn. Could they all be satisfied harmoniously we should all be satisfied once for all and completely. Then doing and dying would coincide throughout and be a perfect pleasure.[41]

The total discharge of tensions, the perfect pleasure, is death. Mingled with Eros, the will to union, is a still more fundamental (though hidden and silent) will to find peace in extinction. Is this not the strange secret that Bacchus and the

Baptist are keeping from Freud in 1910? "They do not cast their eyes down," he writes in the *Leonardo*, "but gaze in mysterious triumph, as if they knew of a great achievement of happiness about which silence must be kept. The familiar smile of fascination leads one to guess that it is a secret of love."[42] Victors over life, they smile with the knowledge of an ultimate fantasy, a terminal satiation. They know the trouble with what the Elizabethans called "dying"—that it isn't really, that it is always only *partial release*. Entire escape would amount to a triumph over biology itself. Leonardo, the putative exception case, is not thus triumphant. The genius turns out to be all-too-human, too, no less encumbered by instinctual self-division than we others. Leonardo's tragedy is the human one of being no apotheosis at all, but merely an "experiment" wherein the countless "*ragioni* of nature force their way into experience."[43]

We are, then, trials and tentatives of nature, not lords and masters, Freud argues. Psychoanalysis has no transcendence to offer, no dignity of the human mind over its natural circumstances, and is therefore not a *gnosis*. (Here, incidentally, is one way to understand the difference between Freudian analysis and the revisionary Jungian variant: the latter is compatible with ideas of a *gnosis* or saving knowledge, the former is not.) Freudian theory and practice refrain from *all* redemptive claims. This certainly includes the modern kind, the claims of Romantic humanism, for all that they form a crucial background to Freud's science. The task he conceives is strictly this: to enable human beings to face the unrectifiable truths of their nature—with grief, with bitter regret, but without false consolation. According to Freud, we are founded on a dualism of instinct which conflicts and encumbers and heaps us inescapably. "Leonardo" is his name in 1910 for what he will later put forth as the involution of the two drives, calling them Eros and death. From the retrospect *Civilization and Its Discontents* provides, Leonardo's sor-

rows may be seen to stand for that antagonism. The tragic
tangle of biology and culture which makes for being human,
makes also, in Freud, for a burden of failure harnessed to the
flesh, an intrinsic pathos of desire.

"I am the spirit that negates," says Mephisto to Faust,

> And rightly so, for all that comes to be
> deserves to perish wretchedly;
> 'Twere better nothing would begin.
> Thus everything that your terms, sin,
> Destruction, evil represent—
> That is my proper element.[44]

The scene is Faust's den. The time is evening. The son of
chaos is explaining himself to the son of light: "I am part of
the part that once was everything," he says,

> Part of the darkness which gave birth to light,
> That haughty light which envies mother night
> Her ancient rank and place and would be king—
> Yet it does not succeed: however it contend,
> It sticks to bodies in the end.[45]

Goethe is the one figure in German literature with whom
Freud unreservedly identified, and it is unsurprising that his
conception of man has its analogue in the Faustian dilemma:

> Two souls, alas, are dwelling in my breast,
> And one is striving to forsake the other.[46]

As the figure of genius, reacher after "the crown of mankind," Faust embodies all that says Yes, all that is culture.
But in his den are two spirits—the other being Mephisto.
Faust's struggle with him is self-division made dramatic, the
bargain between them being actually between heights and
depths in Faust himself.

Here, then, is the precursor of Freud's ultimate myth of
man. Yet Goethe's Faust is redeemed, thereby affirming the

dominion of light over darkness. The spirit of negation is revealed as

> Part of the force which would
> Do evil evermore, and yet creates the good.[47]

For Mephisto is, from the outset, feckless against a greater strength, the human capacity to strive and to affirm. Appropriately, he is a comic figure. Servants typically are in drama and, for all his pretenses, Mephisto is a servant.

But if Freud inherits his mythic dualism of Yes and No from Goethe, in Freud's account the power of Yes has yielded its supremacy. Death is here no subordinate of Eros, but rather at once its sworn enemy and next of kin. As Adrian Leverkühn, Thomas Mann's composer version of Faust, "takes back" Beethoven's Ninth with his *Wehe-klag*, his *Lamentation*, so the Freud of *Civilization and Its Discontents* takes back the Goethean good tidings.

And yet, there is in Freud's later work, as in Mann's, a strain of what Erich Kahler called "immanent transcendence."[48] What remains at the prayerful conclusion of *Doctor Faustus* is what remains at the end of Freud's career—"a hope beyond hopelessness," as Serenus Zeitblom puts it. (Serenus Zeitblom, serene flower of the age, good-hearted, long-winded, the ungenius par excellence whose ungenius is his license to speak. As narrator of *Doctor Faustus*, he tells a thoroughly Freudian parable about the tragedy of German culture: inspired, but poisoned; pledged to beauty, yet the abettor of barbarism.) "Listen to the end," says Zeitblom of the *Doktor Fausti Wehe-klag*, Leverkühn's retort upon Beethoven,

Listen with me: one group of instruments after another retires, and what remains, as the work fades on the air, is the high G of a cello, the last word, the last fainting sound, slowly dying in a pianissimo-fermata. Then nothing more: silence, and night. But that tone which vibrates in the silence, which is no longer there, to which only the spirit hearkens, and which was the voice of mourning, is so no more. It changes its meaning; it abides as a light in the night.[49]

Leverkühn's fainting high G supplants in authority the strident major chords of the Beethoven finale. "Sinners all shall be forgiven," sings the chorus, "and hell shall be no more." Thus Beethoven's Ninth unfolds its promise of transcendent remedy. To this exaltation the *Wehe-klag* offers the fiercest possible rebuke: for in Leverkühn's last testament it is "only out of the sheerly irremediable" that the will to go on, to endure life, may germinate.

Freud's lament, like Leverkühn's, has at its heart the repudiation of every "lullaby about Heaven"[50] with which our nursemaids sought to appease us. He was the unallayed enemy of attempts to comprehend our condition in other than natural terms; *metaphysiches Bedürfnis*, the need for transcendent criteria, he regarded as belonging to the intellectual childhood of mankind. "The moment one inquires about the sense or value of life," he wrote to Marie Bonaparte, "one is sick, since objectively neither of them has any existence."[51] Yet in Freud, as in the *Wehe-klag*, there is "immanent transcendence," the light abiding in the night. "Our god Logos," he called it, the one dream held dear against the welter of his time, for he required a prospect of rationality with which to answer the unprecedented enormities of this century.

Our god Logos. But as Rieff has written, "Freud found intellect only a hope, not a description, and the essential and fundamental thing instinct."[52] As Moses found Canaan only a hope, and the essential and fundamental thing wilderness. In June of 1938, London greeted as a conquering hero the Viennese doctor in flight with his family. Within a few months' time he would install himself, along with books and antique statuary, in the pretty house at 20 Maresfield Gardens, Hampstead. Pessimists, too, have their promised lands; but the suburbs of London were not Freud's. He called his

Canaan by the name of Logos. "We may insist as often as we like," he had written in *The Future of an Illusion* (1927),

that man's intellect is powerless in comparison with his instinctual life, and we may be right in this. Nevertheless, there is something peculiar about this weakness. The voice of the intellect is a soft one, but it does not rest till it has gained a hearing. Finally, after a countless succession of rebuffs, it succeeds. This is one of the few points on which one may be optimistic about the future of mankind, but it is in itself a point of no small importance. And from it one can derive yet other hopes. The primacy of the intellect lies, it is true, in a distant, distant future, but probably not a infinitely distant one.[53]

Pessimists, too, have their promised lands. But what Kafka said about God-fearing Moses applies equally well to the atheist Freud: he failed to get to Canaan not because his life was too short but because it was a human life.

* * *

Conclusion: Bulwarks and Shadows

The dispersion and the reconstitution of the Self.
That's the whole story.   —Charles Baudelaire

In 1769 pilgrims first made their way to Stratford-upon-Avon
to traipse through a half-timbered house in Henley Street
where England's greatest author may have been born, David
Garrick having in that year endowed the place as a shrine.

Travel the hundred fifty kilometers northwest of London
sometime; experience for yourself the lurking phoniness of
Henley Street. Henry James did, and readers of his will recall
a ghostly tale for which Stratford furnished the *donnée.* The
protagonist of James's "The Birthplace," a Mr. Morris Gedge
newly arrived with his wife to assume their duties as live-in
caretakers, finds himself hunted, searched out by a mystery
there—deeper than the bardolotrous fibs he's obliged to pur-
vey to tourists coming through. "Across that threshold,"
Gedge declares for their satisfaction,

He habitually passed; through those low windows, in childhood, He
peered out into the world that He was to make so much happier by
the gift of His genius; over the boards of this floor . . . His little feet
often pattered. . . . In this old chimney-corner, the quaint inglenook
of our ancestors—just there in the far angle, where His little stool

was placed . . . we see the inconceivable child gazing into the blaze of the old oaken logs and making out there pictures and stories. . . .

Gedge understands only too well the false position he is in. Whatever mystic presence there is of "Him" is everywhere and nowhere, not in these particular half-timbers. Even should it happen that Henley Street is not an historical imposture, it is certainly a spiritual irrelevance. Pilgrims fobbed off by an inglenook haven't a purchase on the real secret there. And Gedge is glad of this, for he means to save "Him" from "His" admirers.

Into "The Birthplace" now walk a Mr. and Mrs. B. D. Hayes of New York, and Gedge knows soon enough that these are two "to whom he hadn't to talk, as he phrased it, rot." True votaries unfailingly know one another, and know their difference from the touristically curious who surge to Henley Street.

After all, should the Sunday sentiments of your Aunt Helen and Uncle Jack resemble the passion of Teresa of Avila and John of the Cross? The difference at Stratford between true devotees and the common run is analogous to that between great mystics and ordinary churchgoers. Both call mystery by the same name, yet haven't the same inward relation to it—as Gedge and the tourists call their modern mystery, which is genius, by one name, yet "Shakespeare" doesn't mean in his mouth what it means in theirs. Mr. and Mrs. Hayes provide him with a respite from the fraudulence. For neither nosiness nor biographomania (which is nosiness in excelsis) has coaxed them to this holy ground. The man born there was of an age. But the ghost or familiar spirit or portent of the place is for all time, impalpable but sure, and it is this nimbus "He" makes in the mind, it is this abiding presence, on account of which Mr. and Mrs. B. D. Hayes of New York have come. In this way James telescopes the word "genius" in one of its original meanings—as genius loci, spirit of place—with our own Romantic usage. The aurora of Shakespeare that invests Henley Street James likens by implication to the aurora of genius investing modernity. Such is the revelation that, though it does not take place, has held Gedge, and that the Hayeses have entered into. Ghostly as it is indubitable, this tutelary spirit goes nameless in "The Birthplace." One waits in vain for "Shakespeare" to turn up on any page of James's tale—only "He" and "Him" are there—much as Morris Gedge waits in vain for the revenant of Henley Street to show himself.

The spectral presence is not Shakespeare a man who was born and died in Stratford, but another Shakespeare, illimitable, the auspice of our freedom. Faithless faith is what we have in "Him," the faith Wallace Stevens invoked, beautifully summing up what we've lost and gained, when he wrote: "Modern reality is a reality of decreation, in which our revelations are not the revelations of belief, but the precious portents of our own powers." What Shakespeare has been for us Romantics is just such a portent. By standing as the limit case of greatness, "He" has stood also as a more mysterious and more efficacious name for our freedom. We Romantics have looked no further than Shakespeare, for what could there be beyond "Him"? We Romantics have found in what is human the only glory, the only freedom in an otherwise deterministic universe. "The greatest truth we could hope to discover," says Stevens, "in whatever field we discovered it, is that man's truth is the final resolution of everything." Such has been the quick of our Romantic humanism.

I've argued in this book that an idea of genius presides over modernity. My purpose has been to show how three major modern figures are variously at grips with that idea. Their shared fascination with Leonardo da Vinci—as hero, or fantasy, or conundrum—has been my register throughout. This has been a way of keeping control of what would otherwise be unwieldy, for the question of genius trenches on the vaster question of our freedom.

But how to take hold of this, as elusive a ghost as Shakespeare in Henley Street? Kant is the great modern authority. He argues in his *Critique of Pure Reason* that freedom is an Idea, not a concept; in other words, that it exceeds the competence of knowledge, is without application to anything in our sense experience. Like immortality and God, our freedom resides beyond all possibility of verification.

How, then, do we come to be so fundamentally in possession of the Idea, seeing as it forms no part of knowledge? Man as *phenomenon* belongs to the causal order of nature, answers Kant; man as phenomenon is a mere turnspit, subject to necessary forces; but man as *noumenon* is free. This is to say, as Karl Jaspers puts it in his commentary on Kant, that freedom is "the point where the supersensible is present in this world, where we can, as it were, grasp it in our hands, though we can never know it as something in the world." We are inviolably in possession of an Idea of freedom—we know it to be of our nature—for all that nothing in the causal order can correspond to it, for all that it can therefore never be an object of knowledge like those which come under the purview of the natural sciences.

Observing that great metaphysicians before him had succeeded only in contradicting one another on the basic questions, Kant concludes that these questions must be by their nature insoluble. What he proposes is a turning away from metaphysics, a pensioning off of the old quarrels by showing those quarrels to be based on illusions about the nature and limits of knowledge.

This Kant does in his Transcendental Dialectic by means of the antinomies of pure reason, pairings of opposed, apparently incompatible propositions. His first antinomy posits as thesis that the world has an origin in time and is enclosed by spatial boundaries, and posits as antithesis that the world is without temporal beginnings and is not spatially enclosed. His second antinomy posits that everything in the world is reducible to a primary substance, and posits, in revenge, that no such reduction from the many to the one is possible, that the world admits only of variety.

Consider now his third antinomy, which pairs the proposition that there are no uncaused causes with the contrary proposition that there are uncaused causes. Kant's way of resolving the apparent impasse is to show that while phenomena cannot be uncaused, noumena are not thus subject to the rule of causality. As phenomena we are necessitated, but as noumena we are free. The supersensory, the unconditioned—unamenable to scientific knowledge, yet requisite to human self-understanding—shine forth into our ken. Here in the third antinomy of Kant's Transcendental Dialectic is where we may locate a crucial source of Romantic modernity, that binding curve of cultural energy joining Wordsworth, Byron, Novalis, Hölderlin, Emerson, and Whitman to ourselves. For their Romanticisms flower from the new idea of freedom, a Kantian noumenon or thing-in-itself, a great modern paradox of freedom supplanting the old *liberum arbitrium* affirmed by Scripture and the religious traditions.

Romanticism has given us glories such as *Alsator* and *The Fall of Hyperion;* innocuous notions such as art for art's sake; but also, it must be said, ruthless creeds—the abolition of private property is one example, a higher destiny for Germans another. Romanticisms all. The intellectual sources of this mixed blessing of ours, this checkered Romanticism, are said to lie in four monumental thinkers, Rousseau and Kant, Hamann and Herder, and in a great historical upheaval, the French Revolution. While it is Rousseau and Hamann and Herder, never Kant, who are variously referred to as forefathers of the Romantic, I would argue that it is Kant, bequeathing to the nineteenth century his Ideas (unknowable yet indispensible) of pure reason, who becomes the great philosophical enabler. For it is when his Transcendental Dialectic gets rent asunder—as it will by Fichte, Schelling, and Hegel—that Romanticism results.

According to Kant's philosophy, ideas of God and immortality are no less inherent to us than the idea of freedom. It is precisely this trinity of freedom, immortality, and God that the Romantic philosophers and poets will dismember. Refraining from the Christian God and the Christian immortality, they will claim to make *an adequacy of freedom alone* among those ideas of which Kant said we find ourselves in possession. Romanticism will be just this: *the attempt to make freedom suffice.* But it flourishes in Europe for good and for ill, as we at the end of a century of false prophets know. The worst that human beings can do to one another has been done, and in the worlds Bolshevism and Nazism made, the byword was freedom, whether of the proletariat or of the *Volk,* the perfect freedom that was, in practice, perfect servitude. The outstanding tyrants of our century have been Romantic intellectuals or failed Romantic intellectuals, characteristic products of their time and place, scribbling away in the exile of Zürich or the confinement of Landsberg Prison, determining who shall be made to disappear when the more perfect freedom is secured, the new order instated. The founder of the Cheka, the founder of the Gestapo, these too were Romantics. We prefer to think about the glories, but we had better not neglect the atrocious parodies of greatness our Romanticism has cast up. The founders of the Cheka and of the Gestapo—each was in his day proclaimed a "genius," inevitable Napoleonic appellation, fastened also to Stalin; and, in our own time, to Mao, Castro, Amin, Pol Pot, Qaddafi, Kim Il Sung, Ceauçescu—totalitarian cults of personality being the cult of genius turned to homicidal ends. Thus the word has run its darker course, thriving in debased form, an ideological treacle force-fed to various of the world's poorest and most desperate.

But that ghastliness is another story, not mine to tell here. I have sought in this book to show that the idea of genius— subset of a freedom unyoked from the old God and the old

immortality—has existed to make good the losses our Romantic modernity entails. The genius has stood forth to affirm that, among human lives, some have sacramental shape;
that, among human lives, some put into abeyance the equa-
tion between life and loss. Rilke, whose career exemplifies
much of the Romantic modern, says about Cézanne, the
painter who meant most to him, that he took apples and
bedspreads and wine bottles and forced them "to be beautiful, to stand for the whole world and all joy and all glory." [1]
Such is the post-theological, post-metaphysical role we have
compelled our geniuses into. They make for us a last claim
on the sublime; in them alone, man transcends man. In their
unaccountable creativity—in the sheer gratuitousness of
their works, the marvel that these *are* rather than are not,
and in the ecstatic demand their art places upon us ("You
must change your life!")—we Romantics have looked for and
found the sufficient witness of freedom.

Rilke likened the position of the genius among us to that
of an oarsman he had observed, one of sixteen aboard a large
sailing vessel embarked from the island of Philae:

He sang . . . at quite regular entervals, and by no means always
when exhaustion increased; on the contrary, his song occurred more
than once when all of the rowers were vigorous or even exuberant,
but even then it was the right thing; even then it was appropriate. I
do not know to what extent the mood of our crew communicated
itself to him; they were all behind him, he rarely looked backwards,
and was not affected when he did so. What did seem to influence
him was the pure movement of his feeling when it met the open
distance, in which he was absorbed in a manner half-melancholy,
half-resolute. In him the forward thrust of our vessel and the force
opposed to us were continually held in counterpoise—from time to
time a surplus accumulated: then he sang. The boat overcame the
opposition; but what could not be overcome (was not susceptible of
being overcome) he, the magician, transmuted into a series of long
floating sounds, detached in space, which each appropriated to him-

self. Whilst those about him were always occupied with the most immediate actuality and the overcoming of it, his voice maintained contact with the farthest distance, linking us with it until we felt its power of attraction.[2]

Nowhere, to my mind, is the Romantic sublime better figured than here by perhaps its greatest twentieth-century exemplar. The pure movement of the sublime poet's feeling, when it meets the open distance, overcomes that distance in feeling and in speech, reclaiming transcendence. The Romantic genius, deprived of the old God and the old immortality, with only the assurance of his freedom to orient him, achieves a faithless faith, a natural supernaturalism, an immanent transcendence. Thus, against every precept of a post-theological and post-metaphysical age, man still transcends man. The poet of the sublime accomplishes his link to farthest distances and, in so doing, affiliates us.

So it is that in the voice of genius, belonging wholly and savingly to the order of freedom and not to the order of causality, we find the uncaused cause—gratuitous and unpredictable—that another poet of the sublime, Wordsworth, had invoked as "awful power" from "the mind's abyss" when he crossed the Alps in book 6 of *The Prelude:*

> . . . in such strength
> Of usurpation, when the light of sense
> Goes out, but with a flash that has revealed
> The invisible world, doth greatness make abode.

Along these lines Romanticism responds to the question of where greatness lies. How different from earlier European answers. One did not always have to look so far to certify the reality of freedom. Freedom was not always a Kantian noumenon, inapplicable to matters of fact; freedom was once man's foremost article of evidence, the thing least to be doubted. European man did not always require a specially exalted instance of himself—the genius—to verify that he was free. "That there be a beginning," wrote Saint Augustine in *The City of God*, "man was created, before whom there was nobody."³ Augustine saw in humankind a history of unique and irreducible souls—souls, not selves, immortal and free like their Maker, beginners of things, accomplishers of ends dictated by no necessity. According to Saint Augustine, beginners are what we are; being free, we are here to begin.

But the Bishop of Hippo had the certainty of whence he came and whither he was going, and we do not. Nothing he needed to know was "verification transcendent." A radical freedom, attested by man's nature, was revealed to him, beyond all need of further confirmation, in the first chapter of the first book of Holy Writ, where God makes the light, the land and water, the seed-bearing plant, the sun, moon, and stars, and all the rest, and sees that it is good. But only at the summit of his works, only on the sixth day, does he create a being with choices. The light and darkness, the sun, moon and stars, the birds, beasts and flowers, remain under God's sovereign compulsion. Man alone he does not compel, but rather commands, in recognition of the inherent freedom of man to disobey.⁴ And only then does God find his creation not just good but very good. Here in unassailable Scripture was what Saint Augustine required, the intact, intimately present voice of the Creator, coming from farthest distances, declaring a graceful similitude—that we are beginners in the image of the Absolute Beginner, uncaused causes in the image of the Uncaused Cause.

Like all saints, he had mysteries to contemplate; but not the mystery of what prisoners we are. That has been—distinctively—our modern theme. "How do you break through?" asks Leverkühn, extremest embodiment of the dilemma. "How do you get out into the open?" The modern answer is, "You don't." I have attempted to show that "How do you get out into the open?" is the question my three moderns, Pater, Valéry, and Freud, are asking in their explorations of Leonardo, and that "You don't" is the answer they are, in their several ways, compelled to give. They choose da Vinci to stand for the modern pathos, the all-too-human, our *in*capacity.

I would define this modern pathos as *the devolution from soul to self that it has been the task of Romanticism to remedy.* How do you break through? It would seem that by the sublime, and by no other means, can the Romantic self feel allied to eternity, feel itself to be a soul. What a former time had granted to all in virtue of being human, Romanticism grants uniquely to the genius. Mere men are fragments, riddles, accidents. The genius alone—no longer a fragment or mere self, instead a soul or site of encounter with eternity— guesses riddles, redeems accidents. The genius alone transcends man.

And what comes after this attempt to make freedom suffice? What comes after the characteristic late eighteenth- and nineteenth-century reclamation of soul, known to us from Blake and Wordsworth, Shelley and Keats, from Novalis and Hölderlin, from Emerson and Whitman? What comes after the Romantic sublime?

A perpetual composition and decomposition, a weaving and unweaving, an ongoing dispersal and reconstitution of the self. This is a brief answer; I have attempted in the preceding chapters a fuller response by examining the works of three modern skeptics. What they have fundamentally in common, I find, is *severance from the essential Romantic premise: our freedom.* Pater, Valéry, and Freud show what prisoners we are, whether of the senses, or of the mind's intermittence, or of the instinctual drives.

We are nowadays inclined to speak of Romanticism not just as a literary and philosophical movement but as a perdurable environment of thought and feeling to which we ourselves belong. The majesty of this Romantic culture, as of any other, is to have criticized itself. Consider Blake's or Byron's or Keats' strictures against Wordsworth. Consider Hegel's response to Schelling. Or Melville's to Emerson. Ex-

amples could be multiplied, coming forward into the twentieth and even late twentieth century. It seems probable, to me
at least, that this Romantic self-scrutiny is with us still, and
that movements called modernist and postmodernist will
ultimately be understood as antithetical passages in the un-
finished Romantic story.

Our fiercest of Romantic self-scrutinizers, our most destructive of modernists, Nietzsche, asked, "Was ist vornehm?" He and his Zarathustra answer that all names for
good and evil, all laws, are only parables; that those who are
noble *(vornehm)* create new parables, new tablets of overcoming, while the merely good are satisfied to obey whatever
is inscribed on old tablets, believing it to be "truth." But
what is truth? According to Nietzsche, only those errors
which cannot be refuted:

A mobile army of metaphors, metonyms, anthropomorphisms—
in short, a sum of human relations, which have been enhanced,
transposed and embellished poetically and rhetorically, and which
after long use seem firm, canonical, and obligatory to a people:
truths are illusions about which one has forgotten that this is what
they are; metaphors which are worn-out and without sensuous
power.[5]

The Greek, for example, hangs over himself the tablets of
being first in excellence and of loving none but the friend.
The Persian speaks truly and handles the bow and arrow
well. The Jew honors father and mother, elevating their will
to a sacred law. The Roman conceives a public loyalty for
whose sake all deeds, even dreadful ones, are permitted. The
Christian devises a god of infinite pity, humiliated on a cross,
who by dying abolishes all dominion of death over those who
have faith in him. . . .

Thus their parables become their sacred truths. "A thousand goals have there been so far," Zarathustra declares.
These goals comprise the history of "values"—or opposi-
tions of good and evil, implying our freedom to choose. And

every new "Thou shalt" has its genealogy in some old "Thou shalt" now dishonored, smashed as Abram smashed the idols in Terach's shop. Every new good and evil is an overcoming and ruination of some prior good and evil. Every new good and evil is the telling of a new parable, newly mistaken for truth.[6]

And what of our own times? What tablets did the Romantics hang over themselves, and us? What errors, in other words, could they not refute?

Freedom, genius, the sublime.

Zarathustra avers that no one, so far, has got beyond graven images of one kind or other, mistaken for sacred truths. The *Vornehmheit* of the future, an unexampled nobility, remote from the Romanticist and his idols, will consist in a strength to bear the hardest thought; to shake the nut of existence, hear that it is hollow, and rejoice. So far, says Zarathustra, there has been no such *Übermensch*, only the *Übertier* or overanimal who (unlike his contented fellow beasts) makes history by binding himself to the thousand different "Thou shalts"—Greek, Persian, Jewish, Roman, Christian . . . and now Romantic. "Never yet has there been an overman. Naked I saw both the greatest and the smallest: they are still all-too-similar to each other. Verily, even the greatest I found all-too-human."

Thus spoke Zarathustra, passing by the priests, custodians of a thousand "Thou shalts." As prelude to the overman, Nietzsche's hero laughs to scorn the value of all values hitherto. What have these been, anyhow? Man's stay and prop against nihilism—the disattribution and disesteeming of all values, the dogma of Silenus that everything means nothing, that not to have been born is best. Nihilism obtains when all choices have become meaningless because man has abjured the faith in his freedom, outgrown the logical-metaphysical postulate of an ego or subject as cause of his deeds. The *Übermensch*, overcomer of Romanticism, ruiner of its sacred truths, will no longer require this faith in the subject, nor in these opposite values, good against evil, by which we *Über-tiere* have all-too-humanly sought to ascertain our freedom. The *Wissensdrang* characteristic of every humanism will not beset the overman. He will search out no redemptive meaning to existence, rather love only fate, hanker only for the nuptial ring of rings, everlasting recurrence, nihilistic eternity of the same. He will bear the past no *ressentiment* but rather recreate every "So it was" into an exultant "So I willed it."

In the central section of *Thus Spoke Zarathustra* entitled "On the Vision and the Riddle," Zarathustra says to the pestering dwarf of himself, embodiment of an oleaginous spirit of gravity,

Behold . . . this moment! From this gateway, Moment, a long eternal lane leads *backward:* behind us lies an eternity. Must not whatever *can* walk have walked on this lane before? Must not whatever *can* happen have happened, have been done, have passed by before? And if everything has been there before—what do you think, dwarf, of this moment? And are not all things knotted together so firmly that this moment draws after it *all* that is to come? Therefore—itself too? For whatever *can* walk—in this long lane out *there* too, *must* walk once more. And this slow spider, which crawls in the moonlight, and this moonlight itself, and I and you in the gateway, whispering together, whispering of eternal things—must not all of us have been there before? And return and walk in that other lane, out there, before us, in this long dreadful lane—must we not eternally return?

This is the hardest, most abysmal thought. Only a chanting, glorying, affirming philosopher of the future can bear to think it. Neither Pater, Valéry, nor Freud fits the bill. True, they stand remote from logical-metaphysical illusions: they are all three deep kindred of Nietzsche. But they do not pronounce the Zarathustrian Yes. Acknowledge though they may a metaphysical meaninglessness and an illusoriness of freedom, they lack what Nietzsche called the "Dionysian relationship to existence," exultant roistering *amor fati.*

They do not affirm the mandala of recurrence, *eternal* meaningless determinism of the same.

Such will be the overman's task. No one has accomplished it. No one has loved fate as Zarathustra counseled, hence no one has found the way out of our Romantic modernity. For disillusion does not suffice. The harshly magisterial achievements of Kafka and Beckett no more constitute *amor fati* than did those of Leopardi and Schopenhauer. All are human, all too human from the overman's point of view, and *Thus Spoke Zarathustra* remains what Nietzsche called it—a book for all and none.

With Pater, Valéry, and Freud the sacred truths of Romanticism have entered into crisis. These three are participants in a Romantic waning that has coexisted alongside of the abiding high Romanticisms in, for instance, Yeats, Rilke, Stevens. Taken together, Pater, Valéry, and Freud may be said to represent the lapse from a humanism vested in Romantic ideas. They exhibit, however, nothing like the Nietzschean affirmation of becoming and destruction. Indeed, what strikes most is their distinctly un-Dionysian regret or bereavement.

Greeks, Persians, Hebrews, Romans, Gnostics, Christians—these have in common that they beheld things to believe in, bulwarks in the stream. To that extent, the Romantic is like them. But what remains for lapsed Romantics? Only shadows where the bulwarks were. Pater, Valéry, and Freud are in their Leonardo portraits left with but the apparition of genius, our old sacred truth, to dream on. And yet do not sacred truths have a way of subsisting in the bones of those who lapse from them? And is not a stubborn subsistence evident in these three? We do not know yet what the half-life of Romanticism is. May it be long. May we remain human, all too human a long good while, even if never again to know the like of Ralph Waldo Emerson or Wallace Stevens, Friedrich Hölderlin or Rainer Maria Rilke, Percy Shelley or W. B. Yeats.

Notes

Notes to Introduction

1. Acts of the Apostles 8:9–12. But for a modern account see the late Danilo Kiš's masterly tale "Simon Magus," in *The Encyclopedia of the Dead*, trans. Michael Henry Heim (New York, 1989), 3–24.

2. Friedrich Nietzsche, *Beyond Good and Evil*, trans. Walter Kaufmann (New York, 1966), 160.

3. Friedrich Nietzsche, *The Will to Power*, trans. Walter Kaufmann (New York, 1967), 9.

4. As quoted in Elaine Pagels, *The Gnostic Gospels* (New York, 1979,) 162. The ancient text from which Professor Pagels quotes is Hippolytus's *Refutationis Omnium Haeresium*.

5. Ibid., 158.

6. Ibid., 162.

7. Ibid., 152.

8. Ibid., 161.

9. The best Faust scholarship is still in Eliza M. Butler, *The Myth of the Magus* (Cambridge, 1948) and *The Fortunes of Faust* (Cambridge, 1952), superb books that I am obligated to in my argument as it touches on Faust and the magical tradition.

10. Giovanni Pico della Mirandola, *Oration on the Dignity of Man*, trans. A. Robert Caponigri (Chicago, 1956), 56–57.

11. Ibid., 54.

12. Ibid., 53.

13. Ibid., 57.

14. Ibid., 56.

15. As quoted by E. M. Gombrich in "Leonardo and the Magi-

cians: Polemics and Rivalry," in *New Light on Old Masters* (Chicago, 1986), 73. I have benefited greatly from this essay, and also from Eugenio Garin's "The Universality of Leonardo," in *Science and Civic Life in the Italian Renaissance*, trans. Peter Munz (Garden City, N.Y., 1969), 49–74.

16. Kenneth Clark, *Leonardo da Vinci*, rev. ed. (Middlesex, 1959), 16. For an exhaustive, brilliant examination of the theme of the artist as magician, see Ernst Kris and Otto Kurz, *Legend, Myth, and Magic in the Image of the Artist: An Historical Experiment* (New Haven, Conn., 1979). This book, one of the very greatest examples of Warburgian research, has been for me a constant source of learning, along with Erwin Panofsky's *Idea: A Concept in Art Theory* (Columbia, S.C., 1968).

17. Jules Michelet, *Histoire de France*, vol. 7 (Paris, 1891), 88.

18. I use here the translation that Marguerite Yourcenar and Grace Frick include as a motto to Yourcenar's *The Abyss*, trans. Grace Frick in collaboration with the author (New York, 1976).

19. Friedrich Nietzsche, *Schopenhauer as Educator*, trans. James Hillesheim and Malcolm Simpson (South Bend, Ind., 1965), 78.

20. Arthur Schopenhauer, "On Genius," in *The Will to Live: Selected Writings of Arthur Schopenhauer*, trans. and ed. Richard Taylor (New York, 1962), 321–29 passim. Translation slightly altered.

21. Denis Diderot, "Génie," in the *Encyclopédie ou dictionnaire raisonné des sciences, des arts, et des métiers*, ed. Alain Pons (Paris, 1963), 334–39 passim. Translation mine.

22. Friedrich Nietzsche, *Daybreak: Thoughts on the Prejudices of Morality*, trans. R. J. Hollingdale (Cambridge, 1982), 549–50.

23. Friedrich Nietzsche, *The Gay Science*, trans. Walter Kaufmann (New York, 1974), 273.

Notes to Chapter 1

1. Graham Hough, *The Last Romantics* (London, 1947), 144.

2. I am indebted here to critical insights of Professor Richard Poirier, particularly in *The Performing Self* (New York, 1971) and *The Renewal of Literature: Emersonian Reflections* (New York, 1987).

3. Walter Pater, "Style," in *Appreciations* (London, 1889), 1.

4. Jakob Burckhardt, *Weltgeschichtliche Betrachtungen*, in *Ja-*

kob Burckhardt-Gesamtausgabe, vol. 7 (Stuttgart, 1929), 206. Translation mine.

5. Kenneth Clark, "Walter Pater," in *Moments of Vision* (New York, 1981), 130–42.

6. A journal entry from August 14, 1939. See *Selections from Ralph Waldo Emerson,* ed. Stephen Whicher (Boston, 1957), 135.

7. Friedrich Nietzsche, *The Will to Power,* trans. Walter Kaufmann (New York, 1967), 299.

8. Walter Pater, "The School of Giorgione," in the *Fortnightly Review,* October 1877. Quoted in Donald L. Hill's critical edition of the 1893 text of *The Renaissance* (Berkeley, 1980), 241–42.

9. Thomas Weiskel, *The Romantic Sublime* (Baltimore, 1976), 3.

10. Quoted by Hill, op. cit., 363.

11. Martin Kemp, *Leonardo da Vinci* (Cambridge, Mass., 1981), 26.

12. Harold Bloom, "Walter Pater," in *Figures of Capable Imagination* (New York, 1976), 32–33.

13. Théophile Gautier, "Léonard de Vinci," in *Les dieux et les demi-dieux de la peinture* (Paris, 1864), 19–20.

14. Jules Michelet, Introduction to *Histoire de France, vol. 7* (Paris, 1833–1867), 88–92. As quoted by Hill, op. cit., 363.

15. Heine translated "Les Dieux en Exil," which had appeared in the *Revue des deux mondes* for April 1, 1853, into German later that same year, and it is this second version that Pater consults. See the *Sämtliche Werke,* vol. 8, ed. Adolph Strodtmann (Hamburg, 1861–1869), 209–300. The phrase I quote is translated by Hill, op. cit., 322.

16. A passage that appeared only in the first, unsigned version of "Winckelmann," *Westminster Review* 31 (January 1867): 80–110. Quoted in full by Hill, op. cit., 268.

17. Another suppressed phrase from the *Westminster* "Winckelmann." See Hill, op. cit, 266.

18. Nietzsche, op. cit., 427.

19. Hermann Broch, "James Joyce und die Gegenwart," in *Essays,* vol. 1 (Zürich, 1955), 207.

20. I quote here from Professor Charles Kahn's translation of the fragments, and have been educated in Heraclitus by his splendid commentary. See *The Art and Thought of Heraclitus* (Cambridge, 1979).

21. Sidney Colvin, *Pall Mall Gazette*, March 1, 1873, 12.

22. Friedrich Nietzsche, *The Gay Science*, trans. Walter Kaufmann (New York, 1974), 168.

23. Walter Pater, "Poems by William Morris," *Westminster Review* 34 (October 1868): 300–12. Six of the last seven paragraphs of this unsigned review go to form the conclusion to *The Renaissance;* I quote here from the one that was not reprinted.

24. Nietzsche, *The Will to Power*, 267–70.

Notes to Chapter 2

1. Paul Valéry, *Oeuvres*, vol. 1, (Paris, 1957), 130.

2. Paul Valéry, *The Collected Works of Paul Valéry*, vol. 3 (New York, 1960), 331. (The translator here, to whom my title is owed, is the late Robert Fitzgerald.) [*Oeuvres*, 1:410—*je n'ai pour soif qu'une amour sans mélange. . . .*]

3. *The Collected Works*, 3:339. [*Oeuvres*, vol. 1:413—*Je m'abreuve de moi. . . .*]

4. *Oeuvres*, 1:128.

5. *Oeuvres*, 1:125–26.

6. *Oeuvres*, 1:130.

7. *The Collected Works*, 7:46. [*Oeuvres*, 1:1275—*Car c'est une limite du monde qu'une vérité de cette espèce; il n'est pas permis de s'y établir. Rien de si pur ne peut coexister avec les conditions de la vie.*]

8. *The Collected Works*, 7:192. [*Oeuvres*, 1:1463—*le langage du poète . . . constitue . . .* un effort de l'homme isolé *pour créer un ordre artificiel et idéal, au moyen d'une matière d'origine vulgaire.*]

9. *The Collected Works*, 1:xv. [*Oeuvres*, 1:304—*J'appelle* "monde," *ici, l'ensemble d'incidents, d'injonctions, d'interpellations et de sollicitations de toute espèce et de toute intensité, qui surprennent l'esprit sans l'illuminer en lui-même, qui l'émeuvent en le déconcertant, qui le déplace de plus important vers le moins . . . .*]

10. *The Collected Works*, 8:270. [*Oeuvres*, 1:679—*Il ne consentait pas à écrire sans savoir ce que c'est que d'écrire, et ce que peut signifier cette étrange pratique.*]

11. *The Collected Works*, 8:298. [*Oeuvres*, 1:710—*le "fond" n'est plus* cause *de la forme: il en est l'un des effets. Chaque vers*

devient une entité, qui a ses raisons physiques d'existence. Il est une découverte, une sorte de "vérité" intrinsèque arrachée du hasard. Quant au monde, l'ensemble du réel n'a d'autre excuse d'être que d'offrir au poète de jouer contre lui une partie sublime, perdue d'avance.]

12. *The Collected Works*, 8:395.

13. *The Collected Works*, 6:38. *[Oeuvres, 2:40—Mon dénuement réel engendre une richesse imaginaire: et je suis cette symétrie: je suis l'acte qui annule mes désirs.]*

14. *Oeuvres*, 1:113.

15. *Oeuvres*, 1:113.

16. *The Collected Works*, 8:331.

17. *The Collected Works*, 8:331 [Oeuvres, 1:662—l'esprit n'achève rien par soi-même, ne possède aucun moyen d'en finir avec son activité essentielle, et il n'y a point de pensée qui lui soit une dernière pensée.]*

18. *The Collected Works*, 14:38. *[Oeuvres, 2:500—Parfois je pense; et parfois, je* suis.]

19. *The Collected Works*, 4:57. *[Oeuvres, 2:172—comme dans notre esprit se forment symétriquement les hypothèses, et comme les possibles s'ordonnent et sont énumérés,—ce corps s'exerce dans toutes ses parties, et se combine à lui-même, et se donne forme après forme, et il sort incessamment de soi!]*

20. *The Collected Works*, 4:52. *[Oeuvres, 2:164–165.]*

21. *The Collected Works*, 4:56. *[Oeuvres, 2:171—Voyez-moi ce corps, qui bondit comme la flamme remplace la flamme, voyez comme il foule et piétine ce qui est vrai! Comme il détruit furieusement, joyeusement, le lieu même où il se trouve, et comme il s'enivre de l'excès de ses changements!]*

22. *The Collected Works*, 4:52. *[Oeuvres, 2:168—Pour quoi sont les mortels?—Leur affair est de* connaître? *Et qu'est-ce que* connaître?—*C'est assurément n'être point ce que l'on est.]*

23. *The Collected Works*, 9:79. *[Oeuvres, 1:850—Je ne sais pas aimer quelque personne sans me la rendre si présente à l'esprit qu'elle en devient fort différente de soi-même.]*

24. *The Collected Works*, 15:27. *[Oeuvres, 1:1091—Je comprends à l'extrême ce que l'amour pourrait être. Excès du réel!]*

25. *The Collected Works*, 14:331. *[Oeuvres, 2:752—un seuil éblouissant et infranchissable.]*

26. *The Collected Works*, 4:57. [*Oeuvres*, 2: 172—*de même que nous demandons à notre âme bien des choses pour lesquelles elle n'est pas faite, et que nous en exigeons qu'elle nous éclaire, qu'elle prophétise, qu'elle devine l'avenir, l'adjurant même de découvrir le Dieu,—ainsi le corps qui est là, veut atteindre à une possession entière de soi-même, et à un point de gloire surnaturel! . . . Mais il en est de lui comme de l'âme, pour laquelle le Dieu, et la sagesse, et la profondeur qui lui sont demandés, ne sont et ne peuvent être que des moments, des éclairs, des fragments d'un temps étranger, des bonds déséspérés hors de sa forme. . . .]*

27. *The Collected Works*, 14:259. [*Oeuvres*, 2:696—*ce grand essai éternel et absurde de voir ce qui voit et d'exprimer ce qui exprime.]*

28. *The Collected Works*, 1:410.

29. *Oeuvres*, 1:148. The best translation into English is Howard Moss's *The Cemetery by the Sea* (West Chester, Pa.: Aralia, 1985).

30. *Oeuvres*, 1:149.

31. *The Collected Works*, 14:522. [*Oeuvres*, 2:907—*Dieu a tout fait de rien. Mais le rien perce.]*

32. *Oeuvres*, 1:150.

33. *Oeuvres*, 1:149.

34. *The Collected Works*, 9:190. [*Oeuvres*, 1:565—*Après tout, il doit être assez agréable de se donner à soi-même, et de donner aux gens, par le seul fait de se déboutonner, la sensation de découvrir l'Amérique. Tout le monde sait bien ce que l'on verra; mais il suffit d'ébaucher le geste, tout le monde est ému. C'est la magie de la littérature.]*

35. *Oeuvres*, 1:151.

36. From "Au platane," *Oeuvres*, 1:114.

37. *The Collected Works*, 10:84. [*Oeuvres*, 1:1054—*Le pain des hommes, leur vêtement, leur toit, leurs maux physiques, Dante, ni le Poussin, ni Malebranche n'y peuvent rien.]*

38. *The Collected Works*, 10:88. [*Oeuvres*, 1:1057—*Savons-nous si le pain, quelque jour, si les choses nécessaires à la vie ne seront pas refusées à ces hommes dont la disparition ne troublerait en rien la production de ce pain et de ces choses? On verrait périr tout d'abord tous ceux qui ne peuvent se défendre en se croisant les bras. Tout le reste suivrait ou reviendrait aux tâches matérielles, gagné par la misère montante, et les progrès de cette extermi-*

nation manifesteraient dans le réel, pour quelque suprême observateur, la hiérarchie positive des besoins vrais de la vie humaine la plus simple.]

39. *The Collected Works,* 9:306. *Oeuvres,* 1:886—*[dans une époque du monde où le monde va pensant et méditant de moins en moins, où la civilisation semble, de jour en jour, se réduire au souvenir et aux vestiges que nous gardons de sa richesse multiforme et de sa production intellectuelle libre et surabondante, cependant que la misère, les angoisses, les contraints de tout ordre déprimant ou décourageant les enterprises de l'esprit, Bergson semble déjà appartenir à un âge révolu, et son nom, le dernier grand nom de l'histoire de l'intelligence européenne.]*

40. *The Collected Works,* 10:23. *[Oeuvres,* 1:988—Et nous voyons maintenant que l'abîme de l'histoire et assez grand pour tout le monde. Nous sentons qu'une civilisation a la même fragilité qu'une vie.]*

41. The best insights into Valéry's Faust are still those of Maurice Blanchot in *La Part du Feu* (Paris, 1949), 273–88.

42. *The Collected Works,* 3:34. *[Oeuvres,* 2:298–99—J'ai donc ce grand ouvrage en tête, qui doit finalement me débarrasser tout à fait de moi-même, duquel je suis déjà si détaché. . . . Je veux finir léger, délié à jamais de tout ce qui ressemble à quelque chose . . . comme un voyageur qui a fait abandon de son bagage et marche à l'aventure, sans souci de ce qu'il laisse après soi.]*

43. *The Collected Works,* 3:64. *[Oeuvres,* 2:321–22—Me voici le présent même. Ma personne épouse exactement ma présence, en echange parfait avec quoi qu'il arrive. Point de reste. Il n'y a plus de profondeur. L'infini est défini. Ce qui n'existe pas n'existe plus. Si la connaissance est ce qu'il faut produire par l'esprit pour que SOIT ce qui EST, te voici, FAUST, connaissance pleine et pure, plénitude, accomplissement. Je suis celui que je suis. Je suis au comble de mon art. . . .]*

44. *The Collected Works,* 6:145.
45. *The Collected Works,* 6:108.
46. *The Collected Works,* 6:134–35.
47. *The Collected Works,* 7:58. [Oeuvres, 1:1320.]
48. *The Collected Works,* 9:28. *[Oeuvres,* 1:805—Ce qui m'enchante en lui et me le rend vivant, c'est la conscience de soi-même, de son être tout entier rassemblé dans son attention; conscience*

*pénétrante des opérations de sa pensée; conscience si volontaire et
se précise qu'il fait de son Moi un instrument dont l'infaillibilité
ne dépend que du degré de cette conscience qu'il en a.]*

49. From the first strophe of "Profusion du Soir," in *Oeuvres*,
1:86.

50. *The Collected Works*, 14:482. [*Oeuvres*, 2:876—*Il n'y a
qu'une chose à faire: se refaire. Ce n'est pas simple.]*

51. From the concluding strophe of "La Pythie," in *Oeuvres*,
1:136.

52. *The Collected Works*, 14:269. [*Oeuvres*, 2:704—*Je suis à la
fois au plus haut de la vague et au pied d'elle qui la regarde haute.]*

53. From "Palme," in *Oeuvres*, 1:154. The poem has been unsur-
passably rendered into English by James Merrill; see his *Late Set-
tings* (New York, 1985), 72–74.

54. *The Collected Works*, 9:221. [*Oeuvres*, 1:597.]

55. *The Collected Works*, 8:312. [*Oeuvres*, 1:626—*Il a essayé,
pensai-je, d'élever enfin une page à la puissance du ciel étoilé!]*

57. As quoted in E. M. Cioran, *Valéry Face à ses Idoles* (Paris,
1970), 17.

57. In his introduction to volume 9 of *The Collected Works*, xvi.

58. *The Collected Works*, 15:7.

59. *The Collected Works*, 8:395.

60. *The Collected Works*, 15:8.

61. *The Collected Works*, 15:387–88.

62. I am indebted in what follows to Professor Edward W. Said's
pages on Valéry in *Beginnings: Intention and Method* (New York,
1975).

63. *The Collected Works*, 8:7–8. [*Oeuvres*, 1:1156—*Une telle
érudition ne ferait que fausser l'intention tout hypothétique de cet
essai. Elle ne m'est pas inconnue, mais j'ai surtout à ne pas en
parler, pour ne pas donner à confondre une conjecture relative à
des termes fort généraux, avec des débris extérieurs d'une per-
sonnalité bien évanouie qu'ils nous offrent la certiude de son existence pensante, autant que celle de ne jamais la mieux connaître.]*

64. *The Collected Works*, 8:5. [*Oeuvres*, 1:1155.]

65. *The Collected Works*, 8:34–35. [*Oeuvres*, 1:1176–77—*Des
précipitations ou des lenteurs simulées par les chutes des terres et
des pierres, des courbures massives aux draperies multipliées; des
fumées poussant sur les toits aux arborescences lointaines, aux*

hêtres gazeux des horizons; des poissons aux oiseaux; des étincelles solitaires de la mer aux mille minces miroirs des feuilles de bouleau; des écailles aux éclats marchant sur les golfes; des oreilles et des boucles aux tourbillons figés des coquilles, il va. Il passe de la coquille à l'enroulement de la tumeur des ondes, de la peau des minces étangs à des veines qui la tiédirainent, à des mouvements élémentaires de reptation, aux couleuvres fluides. Il vivifie. L'eau, autour du nageur, il la colle en écharpes, en langes moulant les efforts des muscles. L'air, il le fixe dans le sillage des alouettes en effilochures d'ombre, en fuites mousseuses de bulles que ces routes aériennes et leur fine respiration doivent défaire et laisser à travers les feuillets bleuâtres de l'espace, l'épaisseur du cristal vague de l'espace.]

66. The Collected Works, 8:11. [Oeuvres, 1:1159—Car l'analogie n'est précisément que la faculté de varier les images, de les combiner, de faire coexister la partie de l'une avec la partie de l'autre et d'apercevoir, volontairement ou non, la liason de leurs structures.]

67. The Collected Works, 6:96.

68. The Collected Works, 8:6. [Oeuvres, 1:1155.]

69. The Collected Works, 8:6. [Oeuvres, 1:1155—Je me propose d'imaginer un homme de qui auraient paru des actions tellement distinctes que si je viens à leur supposer une pensée, il n'y en aura pas de plus étendue.]

70. The Collected Works, 8:102. [Oeuvres, 1:1228—L'oeuvre capitale et cachée du plus grand esprit n'est-elle pas de soustraire cette attention substantielle à la lutte des vérités ordinaires?]

71. The Collected Works, 8:70. [Oeuvres, 1:1204—J'aimais dans mes ténèbres la loi intime de ce grand Léonard. Je ne voulais pas de son histoire, ni seulement des productions de sa pensée. . . . De ce front chargé de couronnes, je rêvais seulement à l'amande . . . .]

72. The Collected Works, 8:97–98. [Oeuvres, 1:1225—Le caractère de l'homme est la conscience; et celir de la conscience, une perpétuelle exhaustion, un détachement sans repos et sans exception de tout ce qu'y paraît, quoi qui paraisse. Acte inépuisable, indépendant de la qualité comme de la quantité des choses apparues, et par lequel l'homme de l'esprit doit enfin se réduire sciemment à un refus indéfini d'être quoi que ce soit.]

73. *The Collected Works*, 8:67. *[Oeuvres*, 1:1201—*Quoi de plus séduisant qu'un dieu qui repousse le mystère, qui ne fonde pas sa puissance sur le trouble de notre sens; qui n'adresse pas ses prestiges au plus obscur, au plus tendre, au plus sinistre de nous-mêmes; qui nous force de convenir et non de ployer; et de qui le miracle est de s'éclaircir; la profondeur, une perspective bien déduite? Est-il meilleur marque d'un pouvoir authentique et légitime que de ne pas s'exercer sous un voile?]*

74. *The Collected Works*, 8:99. *[Oeuvres*, 1:1226—*Qu'est-ce qui résiste à l'entrain des sens, à la dissipation des idées, à l'affaiblissement des souvenirs, à la variation lente de l'organisme, à l'action incessante et multiforme de l'univers?]*

75. *The Collected Works*, 8:95.

76. E. M. Cioran, op. cit., 16–17 and passim.

77. *Oeuvres*, 1:146—*l'étrange Toute-Puissance du Néant.*

78. *The Collected Works*, 15:309. *[Oeuvres*, 2:1520—*Pure, c'est-à-dire qui n'est le signe de rien.]*

79. *The Collected Works*, 14:406. *[Oeuvres*, 2:814—*On ne pense réelement à soi et que l'on est soi que quand on ne pense à rien.]*

80. *The Collected Works*, 14:370. *[Oeuvres*, 2:785—*L'object propre, unique et perpétuel de la pensée est:* ce qui n'existe pas.]

81. *The Collected Works*, 8:141. *Oeuvres*, 1:1257.

82. *The Collected Works*, 8:150. *[Oeuvres*, 1:1264—*On pourrait se représenter la philosophie comme l'attitude, l'attente, la contrainte, moyennant lesquelles quelqu'un, parfois, pense sa vie ou vit sa pensée, dans une sorte d'équivalence, ou d'état réversible, entre l'être et le connaître, essayant de suspendre toute expression conventionelle pendant qu'il pressent que s'ordonne et va s'éclairer une combinaison, beaucoup plus précieuse que les autres, du réel qu'il se sent offrir et de celui qu'il peut recevoir.]*

83. *The Collected Works*, 8:117. *[Oeuvres*, 1:1239–40—*On assiste à ce phénomène extraordinaire: le développement même des sciences tend à diminuer la notion du Savoir. Je veux dire que cette partie de la science qui paraissait inébranlable et qui lui était commune avec la philosophie, (c'est-à-dire avec la foi dans l'intelligible et la croyance à la valeur propre des acquisitions de l'esprit), le cède peu à peu à un mode nouveau de concevoir ou d'évaluer le rôle de la connaissance. L'effort de l'intellect ne peut plus être regardé comme convergent vers une limite spirituelle, vers le* Vrai.]

84. *The Collected Works*, 8:135. *[Oeuvres*, 1:1253—*Je dis:* que
la Science est l'ensemble des recettes et procédés qui réussissent
toujours, *et qu'elle va se rapprochant progressivement d'une* table
de correspondances entre nos actes et des phénomènes, *table de
plus en plus nette et riche de telles correspondances, notées dans
les systèmes de notations les plus précis et les plus économiques.*

*L'infallibilité dans la prévision est, en effet, le seul caractère
auquel le moderne reconnaisse une valeur non conventionelle. Il
est tenté de dire:* tout le reste est Littérature. . . .]

85. *The Collected Works*, 8:137–38. *[Oeuvres*, 1:1255—*Le savoir de cette espèce ne s'écarte jamais des actes et des instruments
d'exécution et de contrôle, loin desquels, d'ailleurs,* il n'a point de
sens, *tandis que, fondé sur eux, et s'y référant à chaque instant, il
permet au contraire de refuser tout sens à tout autre savoir. . . .*]

86. Jorge Luis Borges, *Other Inquisitions* (Austin, Tex., 1964),
74.

Notes to Chapter 3

1. This quotation and the previous one are drawn from *The
Letters of Sigmund Freud and Arnold Zweig*, ed. Ernst L. Freud,
trans. Elaine and William Robson-Scott (New York, 1970), 65, 44.

2. *The Letters of Sigmund Freud*, ed. Ernst L. Freud, trans. Tania
and James Stern (New York, 1960), 311. [Sigmund Freud, *Briefe,
1873–1839*, ed. Ernst L. Freud (Frankfurt am Main, 1960), 308—*Ich
kann nicht Optimist sein, unterscheide mich von den Pessimisten,
glaube ich, nur dadurch, dass mich das Böse, Dumme, Unsinnige
nicht aus der Fassung bringt, weil ich's von vorneherein in die
Zusammensetzung der Welt aufgenommen habe.]*

3. Arthur Schopenhauer, "On Genius," in *The Will to Live*, ed.
Richard Taylor (New York, 1962), 329.

4. Sigmund Freud, "Why War?" in *Character and Culture*, ed.
Phillip Rieff (New York, 1962), 143. [Sigmund Freud, *Gesammelte
Werke*, vol. 16, ed. Anna Freud et al., (London, 1950), 22—*läuft
nicht jede Naturwissenschaft auf eine solche Art von Mythologie
hinaus?]*

5. As quoted in Ernest Jones, *The Life and Work of Sigmund
Freud*, vol. 2 (New York, 1955), 177.

6. Sigmund Freud, "Reflections upon War and Death," in *Character and Culture*, 124. *[Gesammelte Werke*, 10:344—*Das Leben*

ist freilich wieder interessant geworden, es hat seinen vollen Inhalt wieder bekommen.]

7. Richard Wollheim, *Sigmund Freud* (New York, 1971), 255.

8. E. M. Cioran, *The Trouble with Being Born*, trans. Richard Howard (New York, 1976), 4.

9. Ibid., 32.

10. Freud, "Reflections upon War and Death," 133. *[Gesammelte Werke, 10:354—Das leben zu ertragen, bleibt ja doch die erste Pflicht aller Lebenden.]*

11. Jürgen Habermas, *Knowledge and Human Interests*, trans. Jeremy J. Shapiro (Boston, 1971), 228, 230.

12. In *Therapy and Technique*, ed. Phillip Rieff (New York, 1963), 254. *[Gesammelte Werke, 16:81–82—Entweder die anstössigen Stellen wurden dick durchgestrichen, so dass sie unleserlich waren; sie konnten dann auch nicht abgeschrieben werden und der nächste Kopist des Buches lieferte einen tadellosen Text, aber an einigen Stellen lückenhaft und vielleicht dort unverständlich. . . . Die Verdrängung verhält sich zu den anderen Abwehrmethoden wie die Auslassung zur Textentstellung, und in den verschiedenen Formen dieser Verfälschung kann man die Analogien zur Mannigfaltigkeit der Ichveränderung finden.]*

13. In *Therapy and Technique*, 256. *[Gesammelte Werke, 16:84—Unsere therapeutische Bemühung pendelt während der Behandlung beständig von einem Stückchen Esanalyse zu einem Stückchen Ichanalyse. Im einen Fall wollen wir etwas vom Es bewusst machen, im anderen etwas am Ich korrigieren. Die entscheidende Tatsache ist nämlich, dass die Abwehrmechanismen gegen einstige Gefahren in der Kur als Widerstände gegen die Heilung wiederkehren.]*

14. In *Therapy and Technique*, 156. *[Gesammelte Werke, 8:478.]*

15. Janet Malcolm, "Six Roses ou Cirrhose?" in *The New Yorker*, January 24, 1983, 103. I have also profited from Malcolm's *Psychoanalysis: The Impossible Profession* (New York, 1981).

16. Sigmund Freud, "Screen Memories," in *The Collected Papers of Sigmund Freud*, vol. 5, ed. James Strachey, (New York, 1959), 69. *[Gesammelte Werke, 1:553–54—Vielleicht ist es überhaupt zweifelhaft, ob wir bewusste Erinnerungen aus der Kindheit haben,*

oder nicht vielmehr bloss an die Kindheit. Unsere Kindheitserinnerungen zeigen uns die ersten Lebensjahre, nicht wie sie waren, sondern wie sie späteren Erweckungszeiten erschienen sind. Zu diesen Zeiten der Erweckung sind die Kindheitserinnerungen nicht, wie man zu sagen gewohnt ist, aufgetaucht, sondern sie sind damals gebildet worden, und eine Reihe von Motiven, denen die Absicht historischer Treue fern liegt, hat diese Bildung sowie die Auswahl der Erinnerungen mitbeeinflusst.]

17. O. Mannoni, *Freud*, trans. Renaud Bruce (New York, 1971), 8.

18. "Analysis of a Phobia in a Five-Year Old Boy," in *The Collected Papers of Sigmund Freud*, vol. 3 (New York, 1959), 246. *[Gesammelte Werke, 7:339—Ein Psychoanalyse ist eben keine tendenzlose, wissenschaftliche Untersuchung, sondern ein therapeutischer Eingriff; sie will an sich nichts beweisen, sondern nur etwas ändern.]*

19. Norman O. Brown, *Life against Death* (Middletown, Conn., 1959), 19.

20. Ibid., 12.

21. Ibid., 19.

22. Sigmund Freud, *The Ego and the Id*, trans. Joan Rivière (New York, 1960), 36. *[Gesammelte Werke, 13:274–75—Indem es sich in solcher Weise der Libido der Objektbesetzungen bemächtigt, sich zum alleinigen Liebesobjekt aufwirft, die Libido des Es desexualisiert oder sublimiert, arbeitet es den Absichten des Eros entgegen, stellt sich in den Dienst der gegnerischen Triebregungen.]*

23. Arthur Schopenhauer, "On Death and Its Relation to the Indestructibility of Our True Nature," in *The Will to Live*, 121.

24. *The Ego and the Id*, 44–45. *[Gesammelte Werke, 13:284–85—Die erotische Komponente hat nach der Sublimierung nicht mehr die Kraft, die ganze hinzugesetze Destruktion zu benden, und diese wird als Aggressions- und Destruktionsneigung frei.]*

25. Sigmund Freud, *Three Essays on the Theory of Sexuality*, trans. James Strachey (New York, 1962), 59.

26. Sigmund Freud, *Beyond the Pleasure Principle*, trans. James Strachey (New York, 1961), 40. *[Gesammelte Werke, 13:48.]*

27. Jones, op. cit., 60.

28. Garsin Kanin, *Hollywood* (New York, 1974), 351.

29. As quoted in Mannoni, op. cit., 168.

30. Sigmund Freud, *Five Lectures on Psycho-Analysis*, trans. James Strachey (New York, 1952), 54. *[Gesammelte Werke, 8:59— Die Plastizität der Sexualkomoponenten, die sich in ihrer Fähigkeit zur Sublimierung kundgibt, mag ja eine grosse Versuchung herstellen, durch deren immer weiter gehende Sublimierung grössere Kultureffekte zu erzielen. Aber so wenig wir darauf rechnen, bei unseren Maschinen mehr als einen gewissen Bruchteil der aufgewendeten Wärme in nutzbare mechanische Arbeit zu verwandeln, so wenig sollten wir es anstreben den Sexualtrieb in seinem ganzen Energieausmass seinen Eigentlichen Zwecken zu entfremden. Es kann nicht gelingen, und wenn die Einschränkung der Sexualität zu weit getrieben werden soll, muss es alle Schädigungen eines Raubbaues mit sich bringen.]*

31. Friedrich Nietzsche, *Thus Spake Zarathustra*, in *The Portable Nietzsche*, ed. and trans. Walter Kaufmann (New York, 1954), 167.

32. *Beyond the Pleasure Principle*, 36. *[Gesammelte Werke, 13:44— Vielen von uns mag es auch schwer werden, auf den Glauben zu verzichten, dass im Menschen selbst ein Trieb zur Vervollkommnung wohnt, der ihn auf seine gegenwärtige Höhe geistiger Leistung und ethischer Sublimierung gebracht hat, und von dem man erwarten darf, dass er seine Entwicklung zum Übermenschen besorgen wird.]*

33. Sigmund Freud, *Civilization and Its Discontents*, trans. James Strachey (New York, 1962), 43. *[Gesammelte Werke, 14:456— Dabei haben wir uns gehütet, dem Vorurteil beizustimmen, Kultur sei gleichbedeutend mit Vervollkommnung, sei der Weg zur Vollkommennheit, die dem Menschen vorgezeichnet ist.]*

34. Friedrich Nietzsche, *The Will to Power*, trans. Walter Kaufmann (New York, 1967), 509.

35. Philip Rieff, *Freud: The Mind of the Moralist* (New York, 1959), 115.

36. Sigmund Freud, *The History of the Psychoanalytic Movement*, ed. Philip Rieff (New York, 1963), 55. Translation slightly altered. Freud's quotation is from the nineteenth-century German playwright Freidrich Hebbel. *[Gesammelte Werke, 10:59–60.]*

37. Sigmund Freud, "On Narcissism: An Introduction," in *Gen-*

eral Psychological Theory, ed. Philip Rieff (New York, 1963), 75. *[Gesammelte Werke, 10:162—die Sublimierung stellt den Ausweg dar, wie die Anforderung erfüllt werden kann, ohne die Verdrängung herbeizuführen.]*

38. Sigmund Freud, "A Difficulty in the Path of Psychoanalysis," as quoted in appendix B of *The Ego and the Id,* 53. *[Gesammelte Werke, 12:6—Das Ich ist ein grosses Reservoir, aus dem die für die Objekte bestimmte Libido ausströmt, und dem sie von den Objekten her wieder zufliesst.]*

39. Freud, *Leonardo da Vinci and a Memory of His Childhood,* trans. Alan Tyson (New York, 1964), 30. *[Gesammelte Werke, 8:147–48—die Libido entzieht sich dem Schicksal der Verdrängung, indem sie sich von Anfang an in Wissbegierde sublimiert und sich zu dem kräftigen Forschertrieb als Vertsärkung schlägt.]*

40. Leo Bersani, *Baudelaire and Freud* (Berkeley, Calif., 1977), 61. I am indebted in what follows to Professor Bersani's account of Freud.

41. George Santayana, "A Long Way Round to Nirvana," in *Some Turns of Thought in Modern Philosophy* (New York, 1933), 99.

42. *Leonardo da Vinci,* 67. *[Gesammelte Werke, 8:189—sie schlagen die Augen nicht nieder, sondern blicken geheimnisvoll triumphierend, als wüssten sie von einem grossen Glückserfolg, von dem man schweigen muss; das bekannte berückende Lächeln lässt ahnen, dass es ein Liebesgeheimnis ist.]*

43. *Leonardo da Vinci,* 87. *[Gesammelte Werke, 8:211—Jedes von uns Menschenwesen entspricht einem der ungezählten Experimente, in denen diese* ragioni *der Natur sich in die Erfahrung drängen.]*

44. *Goethe's Faust,* trans. Walter Kaufmann (New York, 1961), 161.

45. Ibid.

46. Ibid., 145. Translation altered slightly.

47. Ibid., 159.

48. Erich Kahler, "Gedenkrede auf Thomas Mann," in *Die Neue Rundeschau* 67 (1955):547.

49. Thomas Mann, *Doctor Faustus,* trans. H. T. Lowe-Porter (New York, 1948), 491.

50. *Civilization and Its Discontents*, 69. *[Gesammelte Werke, 14:481—Und diesen Streit der Giganten wollen unsere Kinderfrauen beschwichtigen mit dem "Eiapopeia vom Himmel!"]*

51. As quoted in Jones, op. cit., 3:465. *[Briefe, op. cit., 429—Im Moment, da man nach Sinn und Wert des Lebens fragt, ist man krank, denn beides gibt es ja in objektiver Weise nicht.]*

52. Rieff, Introduction to *General Psychological Theory*, op. cit., 10.

53. Sigmund Freud, *The Future of an Illusion*, trans. James Strachey (New York, 1961), 53. *[Gesammelte Werke, 14:377—Wir mögen noch so oft betonen, der menschliche Intellekt sei kraftlos im Vergleich zum menschlichen Triebleben und Recht damit haben. Aber es ist doch etwas Besonderes um diese Schwäche; die Stimme des Intellekts ist leise, aber sie ruht nicht, ehe sie sich Gehör geschafft hat. Am Ende, nach unzählig oft wiederholten Abweisungen, findet sie es doch. Dies ist einer der wenigen Punkte, in denen man für die Zukunft der Menscheit optimistisch sein darf, aber er bedeutet an sich nicht wenig. An ihn kann man noch andere Hoffnungen anknüpfen. Der Primat des Intellekts liegt gewiss in weiter, weiter, aber wahrscheinlich doch nicht in unendlicher Ferne.]*

Notes to Conclusion

1. Rainer Maria Rilke, *Letters on Cézanne*, ed. Clara Rilke, trans. Joel Agee (New York, 1985), 40.

2. "Concerning the Poet," in *Where Silence Reigns: Selected Prose*, trans. G. Craig Houston (New York, 1978), 65–66. "Concerning the Poet" was written at Duino Castle in January 1912 and first published in the *Nachlass* of 1929.

3. As quoted by Hannah Arendt in *The Human Condition* (Chicago, 1958), 177. This Augustinian theme of man the beginner recurs throughout Arendt's work.

4. See Martin Buber's great essay "The Tree of Knowledge" in *Good and Evil* (New York, 1953), 67–80.

5. From a posthumously published early essay, "On Truth and Lie in an Extra-Moral Sense," which excellently sums up *perspectivism*, the epistemological doctrine that there are no facts, only

interpretations, to which Nietzsche will adhere throughout his working life.

6. I have profited from suggestions by Leo Strauss in his "Note on the Plan of Nietzsche's *Beyond Good and Evil*," published in the posthumous volume of Strauss's work, *Studies in Platonic Political Philosophy*, ed. Thomas Pangle (Chicago, 1983), 174–91.

* * *

Bibliography

Pater

Arnold, Matthew. "The Function of Criticism at the Present Time." In *The Complete Prose Works of Matthew Arnold*, vol. 3. Ed. R. H. Super. Ann Arbor: University of Michigan Press, 1960–1977.

Barolsky, Paul. *Walter Pater's Renaissance*. University Park: Pennsylvania State University Press, 1987.

Bloom, Harold. "Late Victorian Poetry and Pater." In *Yeats*. New York: Oxford University Press, 1970.

———. "Marius the Epicurean." In *The Ringers in the Tower*. Chicago: University of Chicago Press, 1971.

———. "Walter Pater." In *Figures of Capable Imagination*. New York: Seabury Press, 1976.

Burke, Kenneth. "Three Adepts of Pure Literature." In *Counter-Statement*. New York: Harcourt, Brace, 1931.

Clark, Kenneth. Introduction to *The Renaissance: Studies in Art and Poetry*, by Walter Pater. London: Fontana/Collins, 1961.

DeLaura, D. J. *Hebrew and Hellene in Victorian England*. Austin: University of Texas Press, 1969.

Dellamora, Richard. *Masculine Desire: The Sexual Politics of Victorian Aestheticism*. Chapel Hill: University of North Carolina Press, 1990.

Donoghue, Denis. "Pater's *Renaissance*." In *England, Their England: Commentaries on English Language and Literature*. New York: Knopf, 1988.

Eliot, T. S. "The Place of Pater." In *The Eighteen-Eighties*. Ed. Walter de la Mare. Cambridge: Cambridge University Press, 1930.

Ellmann, Richard. "Overtures to *Salome.*" In *Oscar Wilde: A Collection of Critical Essays.* Ed. Richard Ellmann. Englewood Cliffs, N.J.: Prentice-Hall, 1969.

Fletcher, Ian. *Walter Pater.* London: Longmans, Green, 1959.

Hopkins, Gerard Manley. *The Poems of Gerard Manley Hopkins.* 4th ed. Ed. W. H. Gardner and N. H. Mackenzie. Oxford: Oxford University Press, 1967.

Hough, Graham. *The Last Romantics.* London: Duckworth, 1949.

Iser, Wolfgang. *Walter Pater: The Aesthetic Moment.* Trans. David Henry Wilson. Cambridge: Cambridge University Press, 1987. (*Walter Pater: Die Autonomie des Ästhetischen.* Tübingen: Niemeyer, 1960.)

Joyce, James. *The Portrait of the Artist as a Young Man.* New York: Viking, 1964. (Orig. pub. 1916.)

Kermode, Frank. *Romantic Image.* London: Routledge and Kegan Paul, 1957.

Levey, Michael. *The Case of Walter Pater.* London: Thames and Hudson, 1978.

Pater, Walter. *New Library Edition of the Works of Walter Pater.* 10 vols. London: Macmillan, 1910.

Poirier, Richard. "Pater, Joyce, Eliot." *James Joyce Quarterly,* 26:1 (Fall, 1988).

Powys, John Cowper. "Walter Pater." In *Visions and Revisions.* New York: Shaw, 1915.

Rilke, Rainer Maria. "Ein Neues Buch von der Renaissance." (A 1902 review of the German translation of Pater's *The Renaissance.*) In vol. 6 of *Sämtliche Werke.* 6 vols. Ed. Ernst Zinn. Wiesbaden: Insel, 1955–1966.

Ruskin, John. *The Queen of the Air: Being a Study of the Greek Myths of Cloud and Storm.* London: Allen, 1883. (Orig. pub. 1869.)

Schapiro, Meyer. "Mr. Berenson's Values." *Encounter* 16 (January 1961): 57–65.

Wilde, Oscar. *Intentions.* In *The Critic as Artist: Critical Writings of Oscar Wilde.* Ed. Richard Ellmann. New York: Random House, 1968. (Orig. pub. 1891.)

Wollheim, Richard. "Walter Pater as a Critic of the Arts." In *On Art and the Mind.* London: Allen Lane, 1973.

Woodring, Carl. *Nature into Art: Cultural Transformations in Nineteenth-Century Britain.* Cambridge, Mass: Harvard University Press, 1989.

Yeats, William Butler. *The Collected Poems of W. B. Yeats.* New York: Macmillan, 1956.

Valéry

Adorno, Theodor W. "Valéry-Proust Museum." In *Prisms.* London: Spearman, 1967. ("Valéry Proust Museum." In *Prismen: Kulturkritik und Gesellschaft.* Berlin: Suhrkamp, 1955.)

Arendt, Hannah. *Thinking.* Vol. 1 of *The Life of the Mind.* New York: Harcourt, Brace, Jovanovich, 1978.

Auden, W. H. "Un Homme d'Esprit." In *Forewords and Afterwords.* Selected by Edward Mendelson. New York: Random House, 1973.

Blanchot, Maurice. *Le Livre à Venir.* Paris: Gallimard, 1959.

———. "Les Carnets de Léonard de Vinci." In *Faux Pas.* Paris: Gallimard, 1943.

———. "Valéry et Faust." In *La Part du Feu.* Paris: Gallimard, 1949.

Borges, Jorge Luis. "Valéry as Symbol." In *Other Inquisitions.* Trans. Ruth L. C. Simms. Austin: University of Texas Press, 1964. (Orig. Spanish pub. 1952.)

Cioran, E. M. "Beyond the Novel." In *The Temptation to Exist.* Trans. Richard Howard. Intro. Susan Sontag. New York: Quadrangle/New York Times Book Co., 1968. ("Au délà du roman." In *La Tentation d'Exister.* Paris: Gallimard, 1956.)

———. *Valéry Face à ses Idoles.* Paris: l'Herne, 1970.

Gass, William H. "Paul Valéry." In *The World within the Word.* New York: Knopf, 1978.

Hytier, Jean. *The Poetics of Paul Valéry.* Trans. Richard Howard. Garden City, N.Y.: Anchor, 1966. (*La Poétique de Valéry.* Paris: Colin, 1953).

———. *Questions de Littérature: Études Valéryennes et Autres.* New York: Columbia University Press, 1967.

Kermode, Frank. "Second Nature." In *Puzzles and Epiphanies.* London: Routledge and Kegan Paul, 1962.

128 • *Bibliography*

Lieberson, Jonathan. "Paul Valéry." In *Varieties*. New York: Weidenfeld and Nicholson, 1988.

Löwith, Karl. *Paul Valéry: Grundzüge seines philosophischen Denkens*. Göttingen: Vandenhoeck and Ruprecht, 1971.

Mallarmé, Stéphane, "Le démon de l'analogie." In *Oeuvres Complètes*. Ed. Henri Mondor and G. Jean Aubry. Paris: Gallimard, 1951.

Merleau-Ponty, Maurice. "L'ontologie cartésienne et l'ontologie d'aujourd'hui: Philosophe et non-philosophe d'après Hegel." *Annuaire du Collège de France* (1961).

———. "What Is Phenomenology?" In *The Essential Writings of Merleau-Ponty*. Ed. Alden L. Fisher. New York: Harcourt, Brace, and World, 1969. ("Préface." In *La Phenomenologie de la Perception*. Paris: Nouvelle Revue Française, Gallimard, 1945.)

Mondor, Henri. *Précocité de Valéry*. Paris: Gallimard, 1948.

———. *Trois Discours pour Paul Valéry*. Paris: Gallimard, 1948.

Pascal, Blaise. *Pensées*. Trans. A. J. Krailsheimer. New York: Penguin, 1966. (*Pensées*. In *Oeuvres Complètes*. Ed. Jean Mesnard. Bruges: Desclée de Brouwer, 1964–1970.) (Orig. pub. 1670.)

Poe, Edgar Allan. *Eureka, a Prose Poem, an Essay on the Material and Spiritual Universe*. San Francisco: Arion, 1991. (Orig. pub. 1848.)

Raymond, Marcel. *Paul Valéry et la Tentation de l'Esprit*. Neuchatel: Baconnière, ca. 1946.

Said, Edward W. "A Meditation on Beginnings." In *Beginnings: Intention and Method*. New York: Basic, 1975.

Sewell, Elizabeth. *Paul Valéry: The Mind in the Mirror*. London: Bowes and Bowes, 1952.

Shattuck, Roger. "Paul Valéry: Sportsman and Barbarian." In *The Innocent Eye: On Modern Literature and the Arts*. New York: Farrar, Straus, and Giroux, 1984.

Stevens, Wallace. "Gloire du long désir, Idées." In *Opus Posthumous*. New York: Knopf, 1957.

Valéry, Paul. *The Collected Works of Paul Valéry*. 15 vols. Gen. ed. Jackson Matthews. Various trans. Bolligen Series 45. New York and Princeton: Pantheon Books and Princeton University Press, 1956–1975. (*Oeuvres de Paul Valéry*. 2 vols. Ed. Jean Hytier. Paris: Gallimard, 1957–1960.)

Warren, Robert Penn. "Pure and Impure Poetry." In *Selected Essays*. New York: Random House, 1958.

Wilson, Edmund. "Paul Valéry." In *Axel's Castle: A Study of the Imaginative Literature of 1870–1930*. New York: Scribner's, 1931.

Freud

Bersani, Leo. *Baudelaire and Freud*. Berkeley: University of California Press, 1977.

———. *The Death of Stéphane Mallarmé*. Cambridge: Cambridge University Press, 1982.

———. "The Other Freud." *Humanities in Society* 1, no. 1 (Winter 1978).

Blackmur, R. P. "Parody and Critique: Mann's *Dr. Faustus*." In *Selected Essays of R. P. Blackmur*. Ed. and intro. Denis Donoghue. New York: Ecco, 1986.

Blanchot, Maurice. "Freud." *La Nouvelle Revue Française*, no. 45 (1956).

Bloom, Harold. "Freud and the Poetic Sublime: A Catastrophe Theory of Creativity." *Antaeus*, nos. 30–31 (Spring 1978).

———. "Freud's Concept of Defense and the Poetic Will." In *The Literary Freud: Mechanisms of Defense and the Poetic Will*. Ed. Joseph H. Smith. New Haven, Conn.: Yale University Press, 1980.

Brown, Norman O. *Life against Death: The Psychoanalytic Meaning of History*. Middletown, Conn.: Wesleyan University Press, 1959.

———. *Love's Body*. New York: Random House, 1966.

Burke, Kenneth. *Dramatism and Development*. Barre, Mass.: Clark University Press, 1972.

———. "Goethe's *Faust*, Part 1." In *Language as Symbolic Action: Essays on Life, Literature, and Method*. Berkeley: University of California Press, 1966.

Cioran, E. M. "Civilized Man: A Portrait." In *The Fall into Time*. Trans. Richard Howard. Intro. Charles Newman. Chicago: Quadrangle, 1970. ("Portrait du civilisé." In *La Chute dans le Temps*. Paris: Gallimard, 1964.)

Clark, Ronald W. *Freud: The Man and the Cause.* London: Paladin Grafton, 1982.

Doolittle, Hilda (HD). *Tribute to Freud.* With unpublished letters by Freud to the author. New York: Pantheon, 1956.

Erikson, Erik H. "The First Psychoanalyst." *Yale Review,* no. 46 (Autumn 1956).

Ferenczi, Sándor. *Final Contributions to the Theory and Technique of Psychoanalysis.* Trans. E. Mosbacher, et al. Ed. Michael Balint. London: Hogarth, 1955.

———. *Further Contributions to the Theory and Technique of Psychoanalysis.* London: Hogarth, 1952.

Freud, Sigmund. *The Standard Edition of the Complete Psychological Works of Sigmund Freud.* 24 vols. Gen. ed. James Strachey. Various trans. London: Hogarth, 1953–1974. (*Gesammelte Werke.* 18 vols. London: Imago, 1940–1968.)

Gass, William H. "The Anatomy of Mind." In *The World within the Word.* New York: Knopf, 1978.

Gay, Peter. *Freud: A Life for Our Time.* New York: Norton, 1988.

———. "Freud and Freedom: On a Fox in Hedgehog's Clothing." In *The Idea of Freedom: Essays in Honour of Isaiah Berlin.* Ed. Alan Ryan. Oxford: Oxford University Press, 1979.

Gombrich, E. M. "Freud's Aesthetics." *Encounter* 26, no. 1 (January 1966): 30–40.

———. "Psychoanalysis and the History of Art." *International Journal of Psychoanalysis,* pt. 4, (1954).

Habermas, Jürgen. "Self-Reflection as Science: Freud's Psychoanalytic Critique of Meaning." In *Knowledge and Human Interests.* Trans. Jeremy J. Shapiro. Boston: Beacon, 1971. ("Selbstreflexion als Wissenschaft: Freuds psychoanalytische Sinnkritik." In *Erkenntnis und Interesse.* Frankfurt am Main: Suhrkamp, 1968.)

Hartman, Geoffrey H. "The Interpreter's Freud." In *Easy Pieces.* New York: Columbia University Press, 1985.

Heller, Erich. "The Taking Back of the Ninth Symphony." In *In the Age of Prose.* Cambridge: Cambridge University Press, 1984.

Jones, Ernest. *The Life and Work of Sigmund Freud.* 3 vols. New York: Basic, 1953–1957.

Laplanche, Jean. *Life and Death in Psychoanalysis.* Trans. and intro. Jeffrey Mehlman. Baltimore, Md.: Johns Hopkins University

Press, 1976. (*Vie et Mort en Psychanalyse.* Paris: Flammarion, 1970.)

Laplanche, Jean, and J.-B. Pontalis. "Fantasme Originaire, Fantasme des Origines, Origine du Fantasme." *Les Temps Modernes,* no. 215 (1964).

——. *The Language of Psychoanalysis.* Trans. Donald Nicholson-Smith. New York: Norton, 1973. (*Vocabulaire de la Psychanalyse.* Paris: P.U.F., 1967.)

Leclaire, Serge, and Jean Laplanche. "L'Inconscient: Etude Psychanalytique." *Les Temps Modernes,* no. 183 (1961).

Lieberson, Jonathan. "Is Psychoanalysis a Science?" In *Varieties.* New York: Weidenfeld and Nicholson, 1988.

Malcolm, Janet. *Psychoanalysis: The Impossible Profession.* New York: Knopf, 1981.

Mann, Thomas. *Doctor Faustus.* Trans. H. T. Lowe-Porter. New York: Knopf, 1948. (*Doktor Faustus.* Stockholm: Bermann-Fischer, 1947.)

——. "Freud and the Future." In *Essays.* New York: Knopf, 1957. ("Freud und die Zukunft." Vienna: Bermann-Fischer, 1936. Delivered as a lecture in celebration of Freud's eightieth birthday, May 8, 1936.)

Murdoch, Iris. "Schopenhauer." In *Metaphysics as a Guide to Morals.* London: Allen Lane, 1992.

Nagel, Thomas. "Freud's Permanent Revolution." *New York Review of Books,* May 12, 1994.

Nemerov, Howard. "Thomas Mann's Faust Novel." In *New and Selected Essays.* Carbondale: Southern Illinois University Press, 1985.

Ricoeur, Paul. *Freud and Philosophy: An Essay on Interpretation.* Trans. Dennis Savage. New Haven, Conn.: Yale University Press, 1970. (*De l'Interprétation: Essai sur Freud.* Paris: Seuil, 1965.)

Rieff, Philip. *The Feeling Intellect: Selected Writings.* Chicago: University of Chicago Press, 1990.

——. *Freud: The Mind of the Moralist.* New York: Viking, 1959.

——. *The Triumph of the Therapeutic: Uses of Faith after Freud.* New York: Harper and Row, 1966.

Sachs, David. "In Fairness to Freud." *Philosophical Review* 98, no. 3 (July 1989).

Safranski, Rüdiger. *Schopenhauer and the Wild Years of Philosophy.* Trans. Ewald Osers. Cambridge, Mass.: Harvard University Press, 1990. (*Schopenhauer und die wilden Jahre der Philosophie.* Munich: Hanser, 1987.)

Santayana, George. "A Long Way Round to Nirvana." In *Some Turns of Thought in Modern Philosophy.* New York: Scribner's, 1933.

Schapiro, Meyer. "Leonardo and Freud: An Art-Historical Study." *Journal of the History of Ideas* 17, no. 2 (April 1956).

Schopenhauer, Arthur. *The World as Will and Representation.* 2 vols. Trans. E. F. J. Payne. New York: Dover, 1966. (*Die Welt als Wille und Vorstellung.* In *Sämtliche Werke.* Vols. 1 and 2. Ed. Paul Deussen. Munich: Piper, 1911–1913.) (Orig. pub. 1819.)

Schorske, Carl E. *Fin-de-Siècle Vienna: Politics and Culture.* New York: Knopf, 1980.

Stokes, Adrian. *A Game that Must Be Lost.* Cheadle: Carcanet Press, 1973.

Storr, Anthony. *Freud.* Oxford: Oxford University Press, 1989.

———. "Genius and Psychoanalysis." In *Genius: The History of an Idea.* Ed. Penelope Murray. Oxford: Blackwell, 1989.

Sulloway, Frank J. *Freud: Biologist of the Mind.* Cambridge, Mass.: Harvard University Press, 1979.

Trilling, Lionel. "The Authentic Unconscious." In *Sincerity and Authenticity.* Cambridge, Mass.: Harvard University Press, 1972.

———. "Freud: Within and beyond Culture." In *Beyond Culture.* New York: Viking, 1965.

Wollheim, Richard. *Freud.* New York: Viking, 1976.

———. *The Mind and Its Depths.* Cambridge, Mass.: Harvard University Press, 1993.

———. "The Tyranny of the Past." In *The Thread of Life.* Cambridge, Mass.: Harvard University Press, 1984.

Yerushalmi, Yosef Hayim. *Freud's Moses: Judaism Terminable and Interminable.* New Haven, Conn.: Yale University Press, 1991.

Leonardo

Barolsky, Paul. *Why Mona Lisa Smiles and Other Tales by Vasari.* University Park: Pennsylvania State University Press, 1991.

Bramly, Serge. *Leonardo: Discovering the Life of Leonardo da Vinci.*

Trans. Sian Reynolds. New York: HarperCollins, 1991. (*Léonard de Vinci*. Paris: Lattès, 1988.)

Burckhardt, Jakob. *The Civilization of the Renaissance in Italy.* 2 vols. Trans. S. G. C. Middlemore. Intro. Benjamin Nelson and Charles Trinkaus. New York: Harper Torchbook, 1959. (*Die Kultur der Renaissance in Italien: Ein Versuch.* Vol. 5 of the *Jakob Burckhardt-Gesamtausgabe.* Ed. Walter Goetz. Stuttgart: Kroner, 1952.) (Orig. pub. 1860.)

Clark, Kenneth. *Leonardo da Vinci.* Rev. ed. Middlesex: Penguin, 1959. (Orig. pub. 1939.)

Garin, Eugenio. "The Universality of Leonardo." In *Science and Civil Life in the Renaissance.* Trans. Peter Munz. Garden City, N.Y.: Doubleday, 1969. ("L'universalità di Leonardo." *Scienza e vita civile nel Rinascimento italiano.* Rome: Laterza, 1965.)

Gautier, Théophile. "Léonard de Vinci." In *Les Dieux et les Demi-Dieux de la Peinture.* With Arsène Houssaye and Paul Saint-Victor. Paris: Morizot, 1864.

Goethe, Johann Wolfgang von. *Observations on Leonardo da Vinci's Celebrated Picture of The Last Supper.* Trans. and intro. G. H. Noehden. London: Booth and Rivington, 1831. ("Joseph Bossi über Leonardo da Vincis Abendmahl zu Mailand." In *Gedenkausgabe der Werke, Briefe und Gespräche,* vol. 13. Ed. Ernst Beutler. Zürich and Stuttgart: Artemis, 1949–1964.) (Orig. pub. 1810.)

Gombrich, E. M. "Leonardo and the Magicians: Polemics and Rivalry." In *New Light on Old Masters.* Chicago: University of Chicago Press, 1986.

Heydenreich, Ludwig. *Leonardo da Vinci.* 2 vols. New York: Macmillan, 1954. (*Leonardo da Vinci.* Basel: Holbein, 1953–1954.)

Jaspers, Karl. "Leonardo as Philosopher." In *Three Essays.* Trans. Karl Manheim. New York: Harcourt, Brace, and World, 1964. (*Lionardo als Philosoph.* Bern: Francke, 1953.)

Kemp, Martin. "From 'Mimesis' to 'Fantasia': The Quattrocento Vocabulary of Creation, Inspiration, and Genius in the Visual Arts." In *Viator* 8 (1977): 347–98.

———. *Leonardo da Vinci.* New Haven, Conn.: Yale University Press, 1989.

———. *Leonardo da Vinci: The Marvellous Works of Nature and Man.* Cambridge, Mass.: Harvard University Press, 1981.

————. "The 'Super-Artist' as Genius." In *Genius: The History of an Idea*. Ed. Penelope Murray. Oxford: Blackwell, 1989.

Klibansky, Raymond, Erwin Panofsky, and Fritz Saxl. *Saturn and Melancholy*. London: Nelson, 1964.

Kris, Ernst, and Otto Kurz. *Legend, Myth, and Magic in the Image of the Artist: A Historical Experiment*. Trans. Alastair Laing and Lottie M. Newman. New Haven, Conn.: Yale University Press, 1979. (*Die Legende vom Kunstler: Ein Historischer Versuch*. Vienna: Krystall, 1934.)

Kristeller, Paul Oskar. " 'Creativity' and 'Tradition.' " In *Journal of the History of Ideas* 44 (1983): 105–13.

————. "The Dignity of Man." In *Renaissance Concepts of Man and Other Essays*. New York: Harper and Row, 1972.

Merejkowski, Dimitri. *The Romance of Leonardo da Vinci: The Forerunner*. Trans. Herbert Trench. New York: Putnam, 1902.

Michelet, Jules. *Renaissance*. Vol. 7 of *Histoire de France*. 16 vols. Paris: Flammarion, 1891. (Vol. 7 orig. pub. 1855.)

Panofsky, Erwin. "Artist, Scientist, Genius: Notes on the 'Renaissance-Dämmerung.' " In *The Renaissance: Six Essays*. Ed. Wallace K. Ferguson. New York: Harper and Row, 1962.

————. *Idea: A Concept in Art Theory*. Trans. Joseph J. S. Peake. Columbia: University of South Carolina Press, 1968. (*Idea: Ein Beitrag zur Begriffsgeschichte der älteren Kunsttheorie*. Leipzig: Teubner, 1924.)

Pedretti, Carlo. *Leonardo: A Study in Chronology and Style*. Berkeley: University of California Press, 1973.

————. *Studi vinciani*. Geneva: Droz, 1957.

Péladan, Joséphin. *La philosophie de Léonard de Vinci d'après ses manuscrits*. Paris: Alcan, 1910.

Santillana, Giorgio di. "Man without Letters." In *Reflections on Men and Ideas*. Cambridge, Mass.: M.I.T. Press, 1968.

Saxl, Fritz. "Science and Art in the Renaissance." In *Lectures*. London: Warburg Institute, 1957.

Séailles, Gabriel. *Léonard de Vinci, l'artiste et le savant*. Paris: Perrin, 1892.

Summers, David. *The Judgment of Sense*. Cambridge: Cambridge University Press, 1987.

Turner, A. Richard. *Inventing Leonardo*. New York: Knopf, 1993.

Vasari, Giorgio. "Leonardo da Vinci." In *Lives of the Artists: A Selection*. Trans. George Bull. Middlesex: Penguin, 1965. (*Le vite de' piu eccellenti pittori, scultori, et architettori*. Ed. Gaetano Milanesi. Florence: Sansoni, 1906.) (Orig. pub. 1550.)

Venturi, Lionello. *La critica e l'arte di Leonardo da Vinci*. Bologna: Zanichelli, 1919.

Vinci, Leonardo da. *The Notebooks of Leonardo da Vinci*. 2 vols. Ed. and trans. Jean Paul Richter. New York: Dover, 1970. (*I manoscritti e i disegni di Leonardo da Vinci*. 5 vols. Rome: Danesi, 1930–1936.)

Wittkover, Rudolf, and Margot Wittkover. *Born under Saturn: The Character and Conduct of Artists: A Documentary History from Antiquity to the French Revolution*. New York: Random House, 1963.

General

Abrams, M. H. *The Mirror and the Lamp: Romantic Theory and the Critical Tradition*. New York: Norton, 1953.

———. *Natural Supernaturalism: Tradition and Revolution in Romantic Literature*. New York: Norton, 1971.

Arendt, Hannah. *The Human Condition*. Chicago: University of Chicago Press, 1958.

———. "What Is Freedom?" In *Between Past and Future*. New York: Viking, 1961.

Barfield, Owen. *Saving the Appearances: A Study in Idolatry*. London: Faber and Faber, 1957.

Bate, Jonathan. "Shakespeare and Original Genius." In *Genius: The History of an Idea*. Ed. Penelope Murray. Oxford: Blackwell, 1989.

Bayley, John. *The Romantic Survival: A Study in Poetic Evolution*. London: Constable, 1957.

Beddow, Michael. "Goethe on Genius." In *Genius: The History of and Idea*. Ed. Penelope Murray, Oxford: Blackwell, 1989.

Benjamin, Walter. "Theses on the Philosophy of History." In *Illuminations*. Trans. Harry Zohn. Ed. and intro. Hannah Arendt. New York: Harcourt, Brace, and World, 1968. ("Geschichtsphilosophische Thesen." In vol. 1 of *Schriften*. Ed. Theodor and

Gretel Adorno. Frankfurt am Main: Surkamp, 1955.) (Orig. pub. 1955.)

Berlin, Isaiah. "The Apotheosis of the Romantic Will: The Revolt against the Myth of an Ideal World." In *The Crooked Timber of Humanity: Chapters in the History of Ideas.* New York: Knopf, 1991.

———. "The Counter-Enlightenment." In *Against the Current: Essays in the History of Ideas.* New York: Viking, 1980.

———. "The Magus of the North." *New York Review of Books,* October 21, 1993.

Blackmur, R. P. "A Critic's Job of Work." In *Selected Essays of R. P. Blackmur.* Ed. and intro. Denis Donoghue. New York: Ecco, 1986.

Bloom, Harold. *Ruin the Sacred Truths: Poetry and Belief from the Bible to the Present.* Cambridge, Mass.: Harvard University Press, 1989.

Boyle, Nicholas. *Goethe: The Poet and the Age.* Oxford: Clarendon, 1991.

Bromwich, David. "Reflections on the Word *Genius.*" In *A Choice of Inheritance.* Cambridge, Mass.: Harvard University Press, 1989.

Burckhardt, Jakob. *Force and Freedom: Reflections on History.* Ed. and intro. James Hastings Nichols. New York: Pantheon, 1943. (*Weltgeschichtliche Betrachtungen.* Vol. 7 of *Jakob Burckhardt-Gesamtausgabe.* Ed. Walter Goetz. Stuttgart: Kroner, 1952.) (Orig. pub. 1905.)

Butler, Eliza M. *The Fortunes of Faust.* Cambridge: Cambridge University Press, 1952.

———. *The Myth of the Magus.* Cambridge: Cambridge University Press, 1948.

Cassirer, Ernst. *Kant's Life and Thought.* Trans. James Haden. Intro. Stephan Körner. New Haven, Conn.: Yale University Press, 1981. (*Kants Leben und Lehre.* Berlin: Cassirer, 1918.)

Cioran, E. M. *The Trouble with Being Born.* Trans. Richard Howard. New York: Viking, 1976. (*De l'Inconvenient d'Etre Né.* Paris: Gallimard, 1973.)

———. "The Undelivered." In *The New Gods.* Trans. Richard Howard. New York: Quadrangle/New York Times Book Co., 1974. ("L'indélivré." In *Le Mauvais Demiurge.* Paris: Gallimard, 1969.)

Currie, Robert. *Genius: An Ideology in Literature.* New York: Schocken, 1974.

Danto, Arthur C. *Nietzsche as Philosopher.* New York: Macmillan, 1965.

Dieckmann, Herbert. "Diderot's Conception of Genius." *The Journal of the History of Ideas,* no. 2 (1941): 151–82.

Dilthey, Wilhelm. "The Dream." In *Wilhelm Dilthey's Philosophy of History.* Ed. William Kluback. New York: Columbia University Press, 1956. (Lecture delivered in 1903, on the author's seventieth birthday.)

Engell, James. *The Creative Imagination: Enlightenment to Romanticism.* Cambridge, Mass.: Harvard University Press, 1981.

Frye, Northrop. *The Modern Century.* Oxford: Oxford University Press, 1967.

Gardiner, Patrick. "Freedom as an Aesthetic Idea." In *The Idea of Freedom: Essays in Honour of Isaiah Berlin.* Ed. Alan Ryan. Oxford: Oxford University Press, 1979.

James, Henry. "The Birthplace." In *The Novels and Tales of Henry James.* Vol. 17. New York: Scribner's, 1909.

Jaspers, Karl. *Kant.* Ed. Hannah Arendt. Trans. Ralph Manheim. New York: Harcourt, Brace, Jovanovich, 1962. (*Kant.* In *Die Grossen Philosophen I.* Munich: Piper, 1957.)

———. *Nietzsche and Christianity.* Trans. E. B. Ashton. Chicago: Regnery, 1961. (*Nietzsche und das Christentum.* Munich: Piper, 1952.)

———. *Nietzsche: An Introduction to the Understanding of His Philosophical Activity.* Trans. Charles Wallroff and Frederick J. Schmitz. Tucson: University of Arizona Press, 1955. (*Nietzsche: Einführung das Verständnis seines Philosophierens.* Berlin and Leipzig: de Gruyter, 1936.)

Jonas, Hans. *The Gnostic Religion: The Message of the Alien God and the Beginnings of Christianity.* Boston: Beacon, 1958.

———. "The Gnostic Syndrome: Typology of Its Thought, Imagination, and Mood." In *Philosophical Essays: From Ancient Creed to Technological Man.* Chicago: University of Chicago Press, 1974.

Jones, Howard Mumford. "The Doctrine of Romantic Genius." In *Revolution and Romanticism.* Cambridge, Mass.: Harvard University Press, 1974.

Kant, Immanuel. *Critique of Pure Reason.* Trans. Norman Kemp Smith. New York: Humanities, 1950. (*Kritik der reinen Vernunft.* Stuttgart: Universal-Bibliothek, 1966.) (Orig. pub. 1781.)

Kaufmann, Walter. *Nietzsche: Philosopher, Psychologist, Antichrist.* Princeton, N.J.: Princeton University Press, 1950.

Kiš, Danilo. "Simon Magus." In *The Encyclopedia of the Dead.* Trans. from the Serbo-Croatian by Michael Henry Heim. New York: Farrar, Straus, and Giroux, 1989.

Koestler, Arthur. *The Act of Creation.* London: Hutchinson, 1964.

Kolakowski, Leszek. *Metaphysical Horror.* Oxford: Blackwell, 1988.

———. *Modernity on Endless Trial.* Chicago: University of Chicago Press, 1990.

Körner, Stephan. *Kant.* Harmondsworth: Penguin, 1955.

Kracauer, Siegfried. *History: The Last Things before the Last.* Oxford: Oxford University Press, 1969.

Lukács, Georg. "On the Nature and Form of the Essay: A Letter to Leo Popper." In *Soul and Form.* Trans. from the German and edited by Anna Bostock. Cambridge, Mass.: M.I.T. Press, 1974. ("Über Wesen und Form des Essays: Ein Brief an Leo Popper." In *Die Seele und die Formen: Essays.* Neuweid: Lüchterhand, 1971.) (Orig. pub. 1911.)

McFarland, Thomas. *Originality and Imagination.* Baltimore, Md.: Johns Hopkins University Press, 1985.

Mann, Thomas. *The Beloved Returns.* Trans. H. T. Lowe-Porter. New York: Knopf, 1940. (*Lotte in Weimar.* Stockholm: Bermann-Fischer, 1939.)

———. "Nietzsche's Philosophy in the Light of Recent History." In *Last Essays.* Trans. Richard Winston and Clara Winston, et al. New York: Knopf, 1958. ("Nietzsche im Lichte unserer Erfahrung." In *Neue Studien.* Stockholm: Bermann-Fischer, 1948.)

Milosz, Czeslaw. *The Land of Ulro.* Trans. from the Polish by Louis Iribarne. New York: Farrar, Straus, and Giroux, 1984.

———. "On Creators." In *Beginning with My Streets: Essays and Recollections.* New York: Farrar, Straus, and Giroux, 1991.

Murray, Penelope. "Poetic Genius and Its Classical Origins." In *Genius: The History of an Idea.* Ed. Penelope Murray. Oxford: Blackwell, 1989.

Nehamas, Alexander. *Nietzsche: Life as Literature.* Cambridge, Mass.: Harvard University Press, 1985.

Nietzsche, Friedrich. *Beyond Good and Evil: Prelude to a Philosophy of the Future.* Trans. Walter Kaufmann. New York: Random House, 1966. (*Jenseits von Gut und Böse.* In *Werke in Drei Bänden,* vol. 2. Ed. Karl Schlechta. Munich: Hanser, 1960.) (Orig. pub. 1886.)

———. *Schopenhauer as Educator.* Trans. James W. Hillesheim and Malcolm R. Simpson. Intro. Eliseo Vivas. South Bend, Ind.: Gateway, 1965. (*Schopenhauer als Erzieher.* In *Werke in Drei Bänden,* vol. 1. Ed. Karl Schlechta. Munich: Hanser, 1960.) (Orig. pub. 1874.)

———. *The Use and Abuse of History.* Trans. Adrian Collins. Indianapolis: Merrill, 1949. (*Von Nützen und Nachteil der Historie für das Leben.* In *Werke in Drei Bänden,* vol. 1. Ed. Karl Schlechta. Munich: Hanser, 1960.) (Orig. pub. 1873.)

Pico, Giovanni, Count of Mirandola. *Oration on the Dignity of Man.* Trans. A. Robert Caponigri. Chicago: Regnery Gateway, 1956. (*De Hominis Dignitate.* Ed. Eugenio Garni. Florence: Vallechi, 1942.) (Orig. pub. 1496.)

Pletsch, Carl. *Young Nietzsche: Becoming a Genius.* New York: Free Press, 1991.

Poirier, Richard. "The Question of Genius." In *The Renewal of Literature: Emersonian Reflections.* New York: Random House, 1987.

Praz, Mario. *The Romantic Agony.* Trans. Angus Davidson. 2d ed. Intro. Frank Kermode. Oxford: Oxford University Press, 1970. (*La carne, la morte, e il diavolo nella letteratura romantica.* Milan: "La Cultura," 1930.)

Rorty, Richard. "The Contingency of Selfhood." In *Contingency, Irony, and Solidarity.* Cambridge: Cambridge University Press, 1989.

Rosen, Stanley. *Nihilism: A Philosophical Essay.* New Haven, Conn.: Yale University Press, 1969.

Rothenberg, Albert. *The Emerging Goddess: The Creative Process in Art, Science, and Other Fields.* Chicago: University of Chicago Press, 1979.

Shattuck, Roger. "The Demon of Originality." In *The Innocent Eye:*

On Modern Literature and the Arts. New York: Farrar, Straus, and Giroux, 1984.

———. "The Tortoise and the Hare: A Study of Valéry, Freud, and Leonardo da Vinci." In The Innocent Eye: On Modern Literature and the Arts. New York: Farrar, Straus, and Giroux, 1984.

Starobinski, Jean. "Criticism and Authority." Trans. A. Cancogni and R. Sieburth. Daedalus 106, no. 4 (1977): 1–16.

Steiner, George. In Bluebeard's Castle: Some Notes towards the Re-definition of Culture. New Haven, Conn.: Yale University Press, 1971.

———. Real Presences. Chicago: University of Chicago Press, 1989.

Storr, Anthony. The School of Genius. London: Deutsch, 1988.

Strauss, Leo. "Correspondence concerning Modernity." (Exchange of letters with Karl Löwith, beginning in 1946.) In Independent Journal of Philosophy/ Revue Indépendante de Philosophie 4:105–19.

———. "The Three Waves of Modernity." In Political Philosophy: Six Essays by Leo Strauss. Ed. Hilail Gildin. Indianapolis and New York: Merrill/Pegasus, 1975. 81–98.

Sutherland, Donald. On, Romanticism. New York: New York University Press, 1971.

Tanner, Michael. "Nietzsche on Genius." In Genius: The History of an Idea. Ed. Penelope Murray. Oxford: Blackwell, 1989.

Tatarkiewicz, Władisław. "Creativity: History of the Concept." In A History of Six Ideas: An Essay in Aesthetics. The Hague: Martinus Nijhoff, 1980.

Trilling, Lionel. "What Is Criticism?" In Literary Criticism: An Introductory Reader. Ed. Lionel Trilling. New York: Holt, Rhinehart, and Winston, 1970.

Voegelin, Eric. Science, Politics, and Gnosticism. Chicago: Regnery, 1968.

Weiskel, Thomas. The Romantic Sublime. Baltimore, Md.: Johns Hopkins University Press, 1976.

White, Hayden. Metahistory: The Historical Imagination in Nineteenth-Century Europe. Baltimore, Md.: Johns Hopkins University Press, 1973.

Williams, Raymond. "The Creative Mind." In The Long Revolution. London: Chatto and Windus, 1961.

———. "Modern." In Keywords: A Vocabulary of Culture and Society. Oxford: Oxford University Press, 1976.

Yates, Frances A. *Giordano Bruno and the Hermetic Tradition.* Chicago: University of Chicago Press, 1964.

Young-Bruehl, Elisabeth. *Creative Characters.* New York: Routledge, 1991.

Yourcenar, Marguerite. *The Abyss.* Trans. Grace Frick in collaboration with author. New York: Farrar, Straus, and Giroux, 1976. (*L'oeuvre au noir.* Paris: Gallimard, 1968.)

Index

About the Author

Benjamin Taylor is a graduate of Haverford College, where he studied Philosophy and French, and of Columbia University, where he earned the doctorate in English and comparative literature. He has taught at Columbia, The New School for Social Research, and each spring term is at Washington University in Saint Louis. His essays and journalism have appeared in *Antaeus, The Los Angeles Times Book Review, Raritan, Threepenny Review, Salmagundi, The Georgia Review, New England Review*, and other publications.

He is the author of a novel, *Tales Out of School.*